CONCILIUM

Religion in the Eighties

CONCILIUM

Concilium 202 (2/1989): Liturgy

CONCILIUM

List of Members

Advisory Committee: Liturgy

MUSIC
AND THE EXPERIENCE
OF GOD

Edited by
Mary Collins,
David Power
and
Mellonee Burnim

T. & T. CLARK LTD
Edinburgh

April 1989
ISBN: 0 567 30082 X

ISSN: 0010-5236

Typeset by C. R. Barber & Partners (Highlands) Ltd, Fort William
Printed by Page Brothers (Norwich) Ltd

Concilium: Published February, April, June, August, October, December.
Subscriptions 1989: UK: £29.95 (including postage and packing); USA: US$49.95
(including air mail postage and packing); Canada: Canadian$64.95 (including air mail
postage and packing); other countries: £29.95 (including postage and packing).

Contents

CONCILIUM 202 Special Column

Claude Geffré

Traditionalism without Lefebvre*

SINCE Mgr Lefebvre's act of schism, the Holy See has made increased efforts to facilitate the re-integration into the Catholic communion of the members of the Fraternity of Saint Pius X who refused to follow Mgr Lefebvre to the point of schism.

We cannot fail to rejoice in the fact that a number of priests, clerics and laymen have withdrawn their support from a schismatic movement which in any case has no future. We could almost reach the point of congratulating ourselves on the blind obstinacy of the old Archbishop of Tulle since his extremism has allowed many of his disciples to open their eyes at last. But why should the joy of reconciliation be tarnished by a number of convergent facts which are alarming? More than twenty years after the Second Vatican Council, we begin to wonder what secret strategy prompts the normalisation of the 'Lefebvre affair'. Has not one of the highest dignitaries of the Roman Church hailed the dissidence of Mgr Lefebvre as a providential event? ... The time seems to have come to speak out on what an increasing number of the faithful, priests and even bishops have been quietly pondering.

Within the dimension of the millions of Catholics who serenely live through the heritage of the Council, and in comparison with the matters of serious urgency which concern the historical responsibility of the Church, one is first and foremost confused by the importance attached to a handful of integralists who seem to be living in the wrong century and who refuse to recognise the

---

All the official texts quoted in this article can be found in Numbers 1966, 1967 and 1969 of Documentation Catholique.

living Tradition of the Church on the pretext of remaining faithful to their own cherished traditions.

One is equally amazed at the 'extremes of patience and indulgence' (these are the very words of John Paul II's Motu proprio 'Ecclesia Dei adflicta' of 2 July 1988) which the Holy See has shown towards Mgr Lefebvre. One could understand that the draft agreement signed by the Bishop of Ecône and Cardinal Ratzinger on 5 May 1988 constituted the last agreed chance of dissuading Mgr Lefebvre from carrying out the episcopal ordinations of his choice. But since Mgr Lefebvre withdrew his signature the following day and carried out his threat, how can we not be disturbed to note that this strange agreement still remains the reference text for the re-integration of the renegades of Ecône and the members of the various religious institutions (Carmelites, Benedictines, Dominicans) who had broken with their Order to join Mgr Lefebvre?

Are we to understand that article 25 of the dogmatic Constitution Lumen Gentium on the obedience due to the ecclesiastical doctrinal authority is the only point to have received the explicit support of Mgr Lefebvre and his disciples (article 2 in the text of the doctrinal declaration of the draft agreement)? Do the other basic teachings of Lumen Gentium and of the great texts on the Church and the world, ecumenism, religious freedom ... form part of those 'points taught by the Second Vatican Council or concerning subsequent reforms of the liturgy and the law, and which seem difficult to reconcile with Tradition' (article 3 of the same doctrinal declaration)? The situation is very ambiguous. Mgr Lefebvre's position at least has the merit of clarity: in his letter to the Holy Father of 2 June 1988 in which he denounced the draft agreement, he repeated that he would do everything to 'protect himself against the spirit of Vatican II and the spirit of Assisi', and that in spite of the Holy See's ban he would proceed with the ordination of bishops 'to further the work which Providence had entrusted to him'.

So Mgr Lefebvre is consistent with himself. He understood that he could not submit to Peter's successor at the same time as pursuing his work, that is fighting by every means against 'the false ecumenism which is behind all the innovations of the Council, in the liturgy, in the new relations of the Church and the world, in the conception of the Church itself (and which) is leading the Church to its ruin and Catholics to apostasy' (Letter of 2 June 1988 to the Holy Father). Now it seems that this impossible pledge has been taken up by a number of intransigeant Catholics who seek with fervent zeal to make Traditionalism without Lefebvre one of the legitimate components of post-conciliar Catholicism.

The Motu proprio (already quoted) decreed the establishment of a new commission, Ecclesia Dei, presided over by Cardinal Mayer: 'A commission

*is instituted which will have as its mission collaboration with the bishops, the
dicasteries of the Roman Curia and other interested parties, with the aim of
facilitating the full ecclesiastical communion of the priests, seminarists,
religious communities or individuals who have up to now had links with the
Fraternity founded by Mgr Lefebvre and who wish to remain united with
Peter's successor in the Catholic Church, preserving their spiritual and
liturgical traditions, in the light of the agreement signed on 5 May by Cardinal
Ratzinger and Mgr Lefebvre.'*

*Why, indeed, in the name of healthy pluralism, should we not see a different
liturgical sensitivity become acceptable (the attachment to Latin, for
example)? But is it merely a question of different 'spiritual and liturgical
traditions', to quote the admirably elliptical formula of the text? There may
well be some doubt in the light of certain disconcerting facts. We will single
out only three. And each time it will be noted that the practice of Roman
proceedings is in line with the draft agreement signed by the Bishop of Ecône
and the Head of the Congregation for the Doctrine of the Faith which is
always invoked as the reference text, both for its doctrinal and its juridical
sections.*

1. We learned through the French integralist newspaper Présent *dated 18
August 1988 of the agreement signed conjointly on 29 June by Cardinal
Mayer (later to become President of the* Ecclesia Dei *Commission) and by
Dom Gérard Calvet, Prior of the Benedictine Monastery of Sainte Madeleine
of Barroux (situated near Avignon, in France). Dom Gérard, at odds for
years with the Benedictine confederation and the undisputed leader of that
citadel of Lefebvrist integralism in France, explained in an interview that
what his community had been asking for since 1983, that is the Mass of Saint
Pius V, the catechism, the sacraments, everything conforming to the secular
tradition of the Church 'was granted to them, without doctrinal compromise,
without concession, without denial.' The two conditions set by the Prior of
Barroux to the signature of this agreement deserve to be quoted in full: '1st.
That this event should not bring discredit on the person of Mgr Lefebvre.
This has been said many times during our discussion with Cardinal Mayer
who has agreed. Besides, is it not due to the tenacity of Mgr. Lefebvre that
this status has been granted to us . . .? 2nd. That no doctrinal or liturgical
compromise should be demanded of us, and that no silence should be imposed
on our anti-modernist preaching.'*

*This re-integration into the Catholic communion 'without doctrinal
compromise' was officially notified by a message from the Congregation for
the Doctrine of the Faith signed on 25 July 1988 by Cardinal Ratzinger and
Cardinal Mayer. The text of such an agreement which in practice sanctions
the inherent direction of the integralist movement of Mgr Lefebvre to the*

exclusion of submission to the Pope provoked the confusion of a certain section of the press which was immediately described as 'progressive'. But why should we be surprised? The text was contained in nuce in the fateful draft agreement co-signed by the founder of Ecône and the Head of the Congregation for the Doctrine of the Faith, and makes no mention at all in its 'doctrinal' section of complete adherence to the teaching of the Second Vatican Council. From this concrete case we can know how in every future case we should understand the 'spiritual and liturgical traditions' discreetly spoken of in the text of the Motu proprio 'Ecclesia Dei adflicta.'

2. Next we must speak of the Fraternity of Saint Peter, founded on 18 July 1988 in the Cistercian Abbey of Hauterive (canton of Fribourg, Switzerland). Its aim was to welcome the priests and seminarists who had broken with Mgr Lefebvre following his act of schism. Here again, why not rejoice whole-heartedly at this initiative which should favour the re-integration into Catholic unity of Lefebvre's former followers? But at the same time, we cannot fail to be struck by its strange resemblance to the Priestly Fraternity of Saint Pius X founded by Mgr Lefebvre. Moreover, it enjoys the same canonical privileges as the said Fraternity, as they are specified in the 'juridical' section of the draft agreement of 5 May 1988. As a 'society of apostolic life' directly linked to the Holy See, it benefits from total autonomy in relation to the episcopal Ordinary of the region.

We begin to wonder how to interpret a declaration of intent like this: 'The Fraternity of Saint Peter will welcome to its heart all priests wishing to serve the Church and souls in a traditional spirit', especially when we remember that the seriousness of the Lefebvre movement stems not from the attachment to the Mass of Saint Pius V, but from a rigid conception of Tradition. And how can we not experience a certain unease when we discover that the new General Superior of the Fraternity of Saint Peter is none other than Abbot Joseph Bisig, for six years the assistant to the General Superior of the Fraternity of Saint Pius X and former Superior for seven years of the integralist seminary of Zaizkofen (Germany)? Must we acknowledge that from now on, in the Catholic Church of 1988, we shall have not only to tolerate but to encourage a 'traditional spirituality' which openly distances itself from the spirit of the Council and the spirit of Assisi?

3. Finally, we must refer to the establishment by decree, dated 28 October, of the Fraternity of Saint Vincent-Ferrier as an institution of consecrated life, obedient to the authority of the Holy See, through the influence of the Ecclesia Dei Commission. They were in fact nine 'Dominican' integralist brothers from Chéméré-le-Roi in Mayenne (France), who had assumed the name, the constitutions, the liturgy and the habit of the Order, but who finally broke with Mgr Lefebvre even before the schism. The decree did not grant them the

designation of 'Friars Preachers', but it provided for the regular life following the practice of the sons of Saint Dominic, the use of the Dominican liturgy from pre-1962 books, and the wearing of the Dominican habit.

While discussions were in progress between the General Master of the Order, the Ecclesia Dei *Commission, the Paris Provincial and the Chéméré group, the General Master learned, at the same time as the Dominican Provincials of France who had been summoned to Rome on 16 November, of the appearance of the decree establishing the said Fraternity on 28 October 1988. Not only was this hasty decision an insult to the General Master of the Order; not only did it create confusion in French public opinion over Dominican identity; but especially it constituted an unprecedented attack on the fundamental right of the Preachers over the centuries. How could we, in effect, concede to a group outside the Order the use of old constitutions and the Dominican liturgy dating from before the liturgical reform of 1962 and therefore completely cut off from the living tradition of the Order? That did not seem to matter. Cardinal Mayer himself came to ordain five brothers from the group, in accordance with the traditional rites, in the Abbey church of Fontgombault on Saturday, 3 December 1988.*

The facts speak for themselves. I already know the argument which says that we must not abandon the ground of a certain tradition to the extreme integralists who have followed Mgr Lefebvre into the schism and that we must prove that his former disciples can be re-integrated into the Church without renouncing their convictions. But we are allowed to ask this question: Is the present pledge of the Vatican—namely, not to allow itself to be outflanked on the right—not exactly the opposite of the pledge of the Second Vatican Council which sought to be in touch with the world and to meet the legitimate aspirations of modern man? The typically conservative measures which I have mentioned cannot in fact be separated from other facts which always lead in the same direction. Let it suffice to recall the progressive neutralisation of the episcopal conferences which was particularly confirmed by the re-integration of the ex-Lefebvrists (the President of the Swiss Episcopal Conference was alone in having the courage to deplore in public 'the lack of clearness of the Vatican regarding the re-integration of certain traditionalist communities'), the setting up of the Brazilian Episcopal Conference, the policy of nominating bishops whose most notorious test was the recent deadlock provoked by the appointments of the titular Archbishops of Cologne and Salzburg.

On the pretext of giving satisfaction to the eternal pre-conciliar nostalgia seekers, we risk discouraging a multitude of the faithful who continue to experience the Second Vatican Council as an event of grace for the Church and the world. It should be possible for the Church to carry out its ministry of forgiveness towards those who refused to follow Mgr Lefebvre into schism without disowning all those (lay people, priests, theologians and bishops) who for more than twenty years had been working without respite to receive the teaching of the Council. Now, the sectarian spirit of certain Roman circles is not only disconcerting the Christians of other churches, but it has already rapidly begun to create 'Christians without a Church.'

Translated by Barrie Mackay

Note that this Special Column, like others in this series, is written under the sole responsibility of the author.

MUSIC AND THE EXPERIENCE OF GOD

Editorial

WHAT CAN readers expect from this investigation of 'Music and Experience of God'? The editors prepared this issue with the intention of promoting conversations among the many specialists who have interests in music and worship: theologians, liturgists, musicologists, and ethnomusicologists. These conversations got under way as soon as the editors began planning the issue. Dr Mellonee Burnim, an ethnomusicologist specialising in religious music, collaborated with the regular editors in the identification of questions to be explored and experts to be consulted. The result is an interdisciplinary exploration of music in communal public religious celebration.

The specialists writing here come from three continents: Europe, Africa, and North America. They reflect on many traditions of ritual music, music of many communities of faith. The believing communities whose traditions they investigate are Christian, Jewish, Muslim, and tribal peoples from Africa, Asia, and North America. What they have in common—the specialists among themselves and with the communities whose traditions they consult—is the conviction that ritual music is powerful, meaningful, mediatorial, and transformative. It is a path for human and divine meeting.

But if ritual music is powerful and transformative, it can also be dangerous; and believing communities have regularly sought to contain the power of music by protocols and prohibitions. Sacred instruments—lute, harp, drum, xylophone, the human voice—and those who play them are accorded special status. As with so many other matters in the sphere of human society and the realm of transcendent mystery, traditions associated with music and the experience of God are filled with ambiguity about women. These are some of the matters explored here in an effort to understand the role music has played in the human experience of God.

Determining the relationship between 'popular' music and 'sacred' music, between music appropriate to the secular realm and music appropriate for religious use, between music as sensual and music as spiritual, are other issues that emerge in the conversation begun here. The distinctions seem to exist most sharply in Judaism, Christianity, and Islam, religions of the Word that took shape under the cultural influences of the Mediterranean Basin. Black African musical traditions show little or no interest in the distinctions, their assumptions, and their implications.

The further one investigates and reflects, the more evident it becomes that the pair 'music and the experience of God' are realities that exist only within cultural systems. The proverb, 'One man's meat is another's poison', comes to mind as we reflect on different experiences of music vis-à-vis grace and transformation. Does the source of discomfort not lie within the man rather than the meat? The well-being occasioned by 'appropriate' religious music and the disintegration caused by 'inappropriate' religious music are matters of real significance in any efforts to understand public worship. A high measure of congruence is intrinsic to the effective workings of any ritual system.

A quarter century after the second Vatican council, the Roman Catholic church finds itself a 'world church' in ways quite different from those that accompanied the European expansionism of the colonial era. Anticipating that 'world church' development, the 1963 Constitution on the Sacred Liturgy pronounced, 'In certain parts of the world, especially mission lands, there are people who have their own musical traditions, and these play a great part in their religious and social life. For this reason *due* importance is to be attached to their music and a *suitable place* (emphasis added) is to be given to it, not only by way of forming their attitudes toward religion, but also where there is question of adapting worship to their native genius . . .' (SC n. 119). This measured affirmation of new possibility is juxtaposed with an affirmation of centuries-old musical traditions of European Christianity. Conditions exist both for creativity and for repression in the interpretation of these affirmations. Something of that tension is reflected also in these pages.

In the final analysis, these tensions identify issues which it is the business of theologians to reflect on. Various claims are made about modes of music, the power of instruments, styles of performance and their suitability for engaging believers in ultimate mystery. How is divine presence mediated in the world? What is the human condition that causes people to aspire to transformative experience? How does music express these realities? A critical theology of music in Christian worship awaits further development. This issue of *Concilium* does not aspire to complete that work. It serves to outline the state of the question. Readers can expect to finish this volume newly alerted to the complexity of music as a human art form and, as a communal prayer form, a path for human and divine meeting.

The first set of articles looks at contemporary problems in liturgical music which are being experienced by those—Christian and Jewish—whose artistic sensibilities were formed in the European cultural milieu. First, Gerard Kock gives an account of the pre-conciliar and post-conciliar efforts to shape the discussion about and to influence the development of music for Catholic worship. He shows how the matter can be cast in terms of the tension latent in trying to balance two assertions of *Sacrosanctum Concilium*. On the one hand it is said that 'The Church indeed approves all forms of true art . . .' and on the other it is claimed that 'sacred music increases in holiness to the degree that it is intimately linked with liturgical action' (SC n. 112.3).

The essay by Peter Jeffery argues the case for the promotion of Gregorian chant in the renewing Roman Catholic liturgy. His position finds strength in the conciliar affirmation that 'other things being equal [Gregorian chant] should be given pride of place in liturgical services' (SC n. 116). Jeffery takes pains to attend to the objections of those who assert chant is neither 'popular' nor suited for vernacular liturgy. He presses a claim for the existential cultural universality of this musical tradition originally shaped in the religious milieu of medieval Europe.

Lawrence Hoffman looks critically at the musical traditions of European Jewry and the virtual demise of these traditions under the cultural circumstances of Reform Jewry in the United States. He identifies the bias toward logocentrism characteristic of religious specialists and their consequent readiness to relegate the musical component of religious worship, indeed, of the experience of God, to an inferior position. Hoffman's analysis of the traditional place of music in synagogue worship and the contemporary struggles over music suggest that Christians and Jews in the North Atlantic world have common questions to address. He reframes the musical discussion in terms of ecclesiology and ministry. He sows seeds for further Christian theological inquiry into the phenomenon of liturgical logocentrism.

The second set of articles explores the musical traditions of tribal Africa as these have been appropriated and re-appropriated for worship by Black African Christians in the United States and in South Africa. Liberation theologian James Cone presents the tradition of Black Spirituals—the music of slavery in the American South—as an expression of a people's response to God's presence in their darkest moments. Cone shows the tradition to be a direct witness to the intimate connection between a people's song and their experience of God. The spiritual power of the music was uncontested: the slavemasters called it dangerous; those who created and performed it were liberated by it.

How does a community's song effect its openness to religious transformation? Mellonee Burnim looks at another part of the black American musical tradition, gospel music, with that question to the fore. She notes that gospel singing is a complex ritual event. Ritual garb, bodily style, emotional range, spatial arrangements and environmental cues support the dominantly vocal performance in an overtly Christian religious setting, where the gospel message is proclaimed through song. It is the combination of many ritual elements that is effective in the mediation of group experience of God's power and presence. The congregation's work is to urge the vocalists to unprecedented peaks of performance; and the new musical heights achieved in their turn transform the congregation by opening up for them new realms of possibility. Both performers and congregation together transcend their ordinary experience and both receive themselves in gratitude as transformed and renewed through the performance. The community's musical work mediates for its members the experience of grace.

David Dargie, a South African priest-musicologist, recounts the communal character of singing/dancing among the Xhosa peoples of South Africa as background for the story of the appearance of European church music in the nineteenth century with the arrival of the missionaries. With this mission tradition of church music came also the phenomenon of 'singing' which was only vocalisation without bodily involvement and the non-traditional use of musical specialists to perform the new music inaccessible to most of the congregation. Dargie tells about a contemporary pastoral effort of the South African Catholic Bishops Conference to encourage the development of a more authentic Xhosa church music which will serve the message of the gospel in the culture of apartheid.

When this second set of essays is read in relation to the first group it is clear that musical and theological perspectives alike are shaped by cultural sensibilities. Those of us whose cultural sensibilities are heir to body/soul and spirit/matter dualism and a hierarchical-emanations cosmology of the ancient Mediterranean world have to come to terms with the evangelical witness of Black African Christians on the mystery of graced embodiment as a communal event.

A third set of articles by ethnomusicologists looks at aspects of ritual musical performance that underscore the communitarian nature of liturgical music. Because ritual music is widely understood to have the power to mediate the meeting of the human with the divine, it is regularly subject to a complex code which channels its power. Ruth Stone looks at the timing code for sounding the call to prayer in a contemporary Islamic setting. The code calls to mind T. S. Eliot's observation that apprehending 'The point of intersection of the timeless with time' is 'the occupation of the saint'. The *muezzin's* sonorous chant signals the existence of such a point five times daily; and those who would be holy interrupt their temporal activity in order to take up the rhythms and sounds of an ancient prayer tradition. The traditional conventions of Islamic 'sound art' also signal in the course of the year that 'point of intersection' which is Ramadan and the once-in-a-lifetime pilgrimage to Mecca. Such Islamic 'sound art' is explicitly distinguished from music, a secular use of sound governed by its own conventions.

The editors asked Ellen Koskoff to look at the way the conventions of ritual music define and express women's roles in corporate religious life. She reports on the musical roles of women in three contemporary settings: orthodox Jewry in the tradition of the Lubavitcher hasidim; shamanism in Korea; and the Iroquois tribe of native Americans. In her exploration of musical conventions she identifies themes of women's social marginality, women's religious superiority, and women's power in spiritual mediation. These often contradictory perspectives have their own intelligibility in their particular socio-religious cosmologies.

Sue Carol DeVale looks at the question of the power and meaning ascribed to ritual musical instruments and to the codes governing their design, their dedication, their care, and their use. The account of the protocols for Javanese and Balinese sacred instruments may initially appear exotic to westerners, but the thoughtful reader will recognise analogous concerns within the western liturgical tradition for the selection of organ builders, the ritual dedication of organs, and the naming and consecration of church bells. Revised rites for these ritual instruments persist in the 1984 Roman Book of Blessings, along with a call for cultural adaptation by national and regional episcopal conferences.

J. H. Kwabena Nketia looks at interactive musical performance in worship among African peoples, noting how ritual music is at times the symbolic expression of people's intention to establish their presence to divine mystery and at other times is primarily the affirmation and re-appropriation of commonly held values and sentiments. Readers familiar with Brevard Childs' classic study *Memory and Tradition in Israel* will find in this discussion of African religious sensibilities echoes of themes characteristic of ritual *anamnesis* in Israel's cult. Nketia also looks at the interplay among musicians themselves, whose interactive performance must sustain the required atmosphere for prayer and sacrifice and also cue the various ritual participants about movement within the ritual process.

Each of the essays by the ethnomusicologists is an invitation to liturgical theologians to do some critical investigation of analogous phenomena in traditions of Christian worship. What are Christian liturgy's timely sounds, its range of 'sound art'? How has the Christian tradition defined women's musical performance? How are liturgical instruments and their performers dedicated to and prepared for a transformative task? What patterns of musical interaction have been characteristic of Christian liturgy? The logocentrism characteristic of Jewish liturgical studies of which Hoffman speaks is by no means confined to Judaism.

The fourth set of articles offers complementary theological reflections on the significance of music in the public worship of the church. Adrien Nocent surveys some of the biblical and patristic developments, noting early expressions of the Latin church's reserve about the relation of music and prayer. He notes further the early development of a working relationship that put music at the service of the Word, and the effort over the centuries to maintain music's diaconal role so that it does not overwhelm the message of salvation thought to be better carried by the Word. Joseph Gelineau looks at the human voice as the instrument of the divine Word calling and the believer's resounding act of faith. The dialogical lyric of faith is seen to be sustained in corporate public worship by a music disciplined to support it.

Finally, in an editorial conclusion, David Power identifies some issues for further investigation which emerge from this collection of essays on music and the experience of God. He takes note of some of the assumptions and implications of positions taken by the authors who contributed to this volume and suggests the need for clarification of the relationship among differing viewpoints. Power judges that the church is only at the start of a critical inquiry about the 'right use of music' in formal worship. Twenty-five years after the call for the reform, renewal, and development of liturgical music to serve the church's public prayer, in the last decade of the century in which Roman Catholicism is indeed becoming a 'world church' caught up in the dialogue of cultures, we find ourselves with new questions we never thought to raise earlier. The situation is created by a genuinely catholic appreciation of culture and a reverence for the mysterious holiness of God which is never contained by our expectations.

Mary Collins

PART I

European Traditions of Liturgical Music

Gerard Kock

Between the Altar and the Choir-loft[1]: Church Music—Liturgy or Art?

Introduction

WHEN GIVING courses and lectures I easily find myself using the terms 'before the Council' and 'after the Council'. Recently I have been realising more and more that part of my audience cannot share this comparison. They belong to a later generation than myself and can barely imagine, if at all, what it was like before the Council. For me and my contemporaries the word 'Council' still carries the overtones of 'new' and 'aggiornamento'. But it is more than twenty-five years since Pope Paul VI put his signature to the Constitution on the Sacred Liturgy on 4 December 1963.

Meanwhile, a quarter of a century does not seem long enough for the fundamental insights of Vatican II to be able to penetrate and become the common heritage both in general and in all their consequences. Genuine liturgical renewal seems a laborious process that is only realised in movement and counter-movement—in steps forward and steps back. This is the same at all levels of the Church.

If this applies to the liturgy in general, then it certainly applies too to music in the renewed liturgy. In this article I would like to describe something of that stirring twenty-five years' history, and to do so as the history of the dilemma between the altar and the choir-loft. At the Council itself, but also in the years that have followed, people have been looking for the balance between the demands made by the liturgy—the altar—and the aspirations of church music, symbolised here by the choir-loft.

Church music at the Council

One thing that no longer surprises us so much now, but was certainly striking twenty-five years ago, is the fact that the Council wanted to devote so much attention to music in the liturgy. In the constitution on the liturgy a whole chapter is devoted to church music, and this chapter is not much shorter than that on the eucharist. This sixth chapter, *De musica sacra*, when read within the context of the entire constitution, makes clear that the Council is opening up an entirely new perspective with regard to music. Here too, as with the whole of the liturgy, it was a sharp turn-around.

If you were to read the ten articles of this sixth chapter (arts. 112–121) for the first time today, it is not inconceivable that you should miss what was new and revolutionary. Commentaries written at the time would alert you to this, but otherwise it would perhaps escape you.

The core of the whole chapter is certainly article 112. Here there is mention of a clear revaluation of the function of music in the liturgy. Within the liturgy music is no longer something accidental for embellishment or ornament but it has become an essential and integral part of the liturgy itself. Music is itself liturgy.

Characteristic for this revaluation is the language that is used whenever the Council talks about church music. Pius X and Pius XI still talked of church music as *umile ancilla* and *nobilissima ancilla*. When the constitution defines the function of church music it talks of a *munus ministeriale*, a ministerial function, in which any trace of depreciation has disappeared.

Perhaps still more startling than this revaluation was and is the way in which the constitution defines the close relationship between music and liturgy. In article 112 it states: 'Therefore sacred music is to be considered the more holy, the more closely connected it is with the liturgical action'. Helmut Hucke calls this fundamental statement revolutionary since it elevates not an internal musical and aesthetic factor but a liturgical factor to be the criterion for church music.[2]

Within the liturgy music functions as a form of applied art. It is music and as such can be judged on its artistic value. But alongside this it is equally liturgy. Demands that one makes of liturgy in general apply also to its music. Artistic expression on the one hand, an element in the liturgy on the other: music in the liturgy continually faces us with the dilemma of which of these two factors should bear the greatest weight.

This tension between 'liturgy' and 'art' is not something that sprang up today or yesterday. It existed right from the first centuries of Christianity. This is confirmed by K. J. Fellerer in his *Geschichte der katholischen Kirchenmusik*: 'Everywhere that art was given a limited, clearly defined task there loomed the tension between this task on the one hand and on the other the manner in which this task was interpreted ... Emphasis on the liturgical aspect and emphasis on the musical aspect are antitheses which over the centuries have given a particular stamp to the process of development of church music'.[3]

The criterion quoted above from article 112 makes it absolutely clear how the renewal of Vatican II, which is intended to be a return to the sources, emphasises the liturgical aspect again and does so very strongly. Although the Council champions church music as 'true art which [has] the requisite qualities', it is clear that it sees church music in the first place as liturgy and only in the second place as art.

From this decision on the preference for church music as liturgy all kinds of practical consequences follow. Thus it is striking that nowhere does the Council express a value judgment over which musical style should be adopted: this is in contrast to the popes, who since Pius X, have repeatedly stated a preference for a particular style of church music. Although a certain precedence is accorded to Gregorian chant as the Roman liturgy's own chant, no single musical style is certified as the one true style.

Beyond this, newly acquired insights in the field of the liturgy in general are applied quite consistently to church music too: since the Council worship is once again worship of the entire community gathered together, so too music must be something belonging to everyone and no longer a privilege for the choir alone; the liturgical renewal's favourite term *participatio actuosa* (active participation) turns up repeatedly in the sixth chapter (arts. 113, 114, 118, and 121); and what the Council determined with regard to the use of the vernacular, the division of functions, the concern for simplicity, clarity, and acculturation is to apply to music too.

Even twenty-five years later one can still be surprised at how such a turn-about in principle was in fact possible. In his commentary on the constitution Josef Jungmann lifts a corner of the veil that hides the way things went. He indicates that this sixth chapter was preceded by a first draft which was put together by a subcommission, entirely consisting of professional musicians. They were primarily intent on securing the importance of music and its artistic worth. Even after a revision that placed a little more emphasis on the pastoral and liturgical aspect, the chapter still did not find favour in the eyes of the Council fathers. A complete overhaul had finally to be decided on in which both the value of church music and its liturgical character was stressed even more strongly.[4] The conclusion is clear: the tension between the altar (liturgy) and the choir-loft (music as art) was plainly decided by the Council in favour of the altar.

Church music after the Council

Despite what in our opinion is the clear statement of the Council the dilemma between liturgy and art has continued to dominate the world of church music until today. The more or less silent witnesses of this are the laborious realisation of some post-conciliar documents such as the instruction *Musicam sacram* as well as the emergence of two international associations for church music with contrasting positions and the often high level of discussion and disagreement in the pastoral field.

(a) The instruction Musicam sacram

An instruction on church music appeared in March 1967. Its aim was to develop further the Council's general guidelines with regard to music in the liturgy. When it finally appeared it was generally greeted as a disappointing and confusing document. It is clearly the result of a compromise in which the most contradictory tendencies can find confirmation of the rightness of their cause. What is it all about? In contrast to the sixth chapter of the constitution on the liturgy what is involved here is a document which was originally conceived from the liturgical angle. Gradually, however, more and more objections to that first draft were registered on the part of church musicians. The long and laborious history of the document's genesis speaks for itself.

The first draft was ready in February 1965. After thorough consultation and deliberation the Council for the Implementation of the Constitution on the Liturgy approved a fifth version at the end of that year (2 December 1965) and forwarded it. Soon it became known that various influential church musicians were raising great difficulties with different Roman offices. They feared for the heritage of church music setting Latin words. All in all it was to be more than a year before the instruction was published. It had meanwhile run through ten drafts. The final text diverged quite a bit from the original one. 'Through the shortsightedness of some influential church musicians the instruction was delayed and weakened.'[5]

At the press conference held on 7 March 1967 for the publication of this instruction Annibale Bugnini, secretary of the Council for the Implementation of the Constitution on the Liturgy, said: 'The instruction has been rewritten several times in order to bring the insights that are valid today in the liturgical field into some kind of agreement with those concerning music as art which, following the venerable tradition of the Roman Church, stands in the service of the liturgy'.[6]

Earlier the pope himself, in an address to members of the liturgical council, had indicated difficulties in the genesis of this instruction. At the conclusion of this address the pope expressed the hope that the forthcoming instruction 'will bring a new co-operation between these two splendid expressions of the human spirit, prayer and art'.[7]

That co-operation between prayer and art was as yet to seem a vain hope. The struggle for authority between the liturgy on the one hand and church music on the other, the tension between altar and choir-loft was to continue and persist. The opposing powers which had delayed and made more difficult the emergence of a clear instruction were to become more strongly organised and come to oppose each other even more intensely in the future.

(b) Two associations for church music

More or less at the time of the Council two international associations for church music came into being, independently of each other: CIMS and Universa Laus. Before describing how these associations are the direct opposite of each other and how each of them occupies its own place within the area of tension between art and liturgy it is perhaps necessary to gain a little closer acquaintance with each of them.

CIMS

In order to guarantee the best possible implementation of the conciliar and post-conciliar guidelines with regard to church music and in order to bring together all who had the interests of church music at heart Pope Paul VI on 22 November 1963 (and thus while the Council was still sitting) set up an international association for church music. It was to enter history under the name *Consociatio Internationalis Musicae Sacrae*, or CIMS for short.

Anyone who wanted to belong to this association had to satisfy a strict set of criteria. CIMS wanted to make sure that only genuine professional musicians were admitted to its ranks. Alongside the institutes and associations for church music recognised by the Holy See or the competent ecclesiastical authority, individuals could also belong, but only if they satisfied the conditions laid down by the executive. Some of the great names from this circle are J. Chailley, R. Lenaerts, J. Lennards, J. Overath, F. Romita, J. Schmit and R. Schuler.

One of the activities which brought CIMS into the limelight after its establishment in 1963 was the holding under its responsibility of international congresses for church music. Before 1963 similar congresses had taken place, in Rome in 1950, Vienna in 1954, Paris in 1957, and Cologne in 1961; but after 1963 the organisation of these was entrusted to CIMS and they were held in Chicago and Milwaukee in 1966, in Salzburg in 1974, in Bonnin 1980 and in Rome in 1985. Alongside these international congresses CIMS also organised smaller meetings or symposia for particular language groups. Since 1964 CIMS has had its own journal, *Musicae sacrae ministerium*, appearing several times (or only once) a year.

Universa Laus

Alongside this official ecclesiastical association for church music there is another international association which is particularly concerned with church music, the study group Universa Laus. It came into being roughly a year before CIMS, in 1962, on the personal initiative of several priests and lay-people from Europe who wanted to take an interest in the introduction of the vernacular into the liturgy and church music.

A few years later it seemed useful to give this independent study group a somewhat more official status in order that all who wanted could take part in its work and study. Universa Laus was officially established on 21 April 1966. Its aim was and is to be a study group that offers all who are interested in questions concerning the liturgy and liturgical music the opportunity to meet, to exchange information, to share ideas and to work together: moreover from the start it has been ecumenical in design.

Anyone who is engaged in or interested in musical and liturgical questions relating to the renewal of the liturgy can become a member of this association: liturgists, musicologists, teachers, poets, composers, conductors and organists. There is also collective membership. Names from the first beginnings include J. Gelineau, H. Hucke, B. Buijbers and E. Quack.

Universa Laus holds meetings nearly every year, some by invitation for a limited circle, and alongside these international congresses such as those at Fribourg, Switzerland, in 1965, Pamplona in 1967, Turin in 1969, Essen in 1971, Strasbourg in 1974, London in 1978. Since 1967 the UL Bulletin has appeared. Before that and alongside it members of UL published in Italian *Il canto dell' Assemblea*, in French *L'église qui chante*, in Flemish *Adem*, and in German *Musik und Altar* (which ceased publication in 1972).

CIMS and Universa Laus: each other's antithesis

CIMS and Universa Laus differ in the ways in which they came into being, in their composition, in their fields of interest and in their histories, but both have more or less the same aim in view: carefully to watch and support the new situation in which church music finds itself after the Council. In itself, even differences in subjects of concern (for example Latin or vernacular) and approach need not have been divisive; both groups could have complemented and enriched each other. But this did not happen. Instead each distanced itself ever more from the other to the extent that one can rightly talk of a controversy. In my 1980 thesis I concentrated in detail on significant moments in the history of both movements when this controversy came clearly to light. I also analysed in detail the points of opposition between the two groups.

What interests us in the context of this article is the question of how each of these two groups is to be placed on either side of the tension between liturgy and art, between altar and choir-loft. On the basis of the investigation I carried out I think this is justified, although I hasten to add that it is here naturally a question of emphasis and nuance. To give priority to church music as art does not of course mean to say that one overlooks the liturgical aspect, and vice versa.

With this reservation at the back of my mind, I think that in CIMS one can see the representative of the choir-loft. It sees church music in the first place as music. As such this must always have a certain artistic value. Thus, for CIMS, aesthetics provides one of the principal criteria that music in worship must meet. Church music must above all be true art. CIMS regards it as one of its chief tasks to foster and defend church music as art. Performances of classical and contemporary works by the best choirs and musicians always form an established part of the programme of its congresses and meetings.

The glory of God is for the CIMS *the* argument whereby it provides theological support for its position. And if you make the *gloria Dei* the real and only point of the liturgy and its music (the Council always talks of God being glorified and men and women being sanctified in the same breath), the conclusion is quickly drawn: the best and most artistic that men and women have to offer God is only just good enough.

In contrast to CIMS is the outlook of Universa Laus. In the model I have been using it represents the altar, since for Universa Laus church music is first and foremost liturgy. The first question it asks of music is not: 'Is it justified aesthetically?' but: 'Is it liturgically functional?' (Compare art. 112 of the liturgical constitution.) And here being functional should be understood as a way of being adapted: adapted to the liturgy and its special rites, but also adapted to the assembled community that is celebrating liturgy here and now. Illustrative in this context are the questions with which Universa Laus has been occupied over the course of the years:

'Which music goes with which rite?' 'How does music work as communication?' 'What is the symbolic significance of singing, of listening? and in this age of the mass media?' 'What does celebration mean in contemporary society?'

Because Universa Laus sees the best guarantee for functional adaptation to the liturgy in new music using the vernacular, that is where its efforts and interest have been concentrated.

(c) In the normal pastoral context

From the above one could conclude that the debate 'between altar and choir-loft' was simply being conducted at the top level in the Church. Nothing is less true, as everybody's own experience teaches. It was not so long ago that I myself came across an example that many will certainly find recognisable.

A parish had existed for fifty years. Just when it was on the point of celebrating fifty years of mutual solidarity among its members a disagreement arose between two prominent groups within it: the choir and the liturgy committee. The choir wanted to seize the opportunity of this jubilee to display something extra special: a polyphonic setting of the ordinary of the Mass in Latin, preferably by Mozart with orchestral accompaniment. It was, after all, a celebration.

The liturgy committee was not at all happy with this proposal. A Latin Mass, their argument ran, turned those present into an audience, and this was inadmissible when one was proposing to celebrate a feast together. The liturgy committee's preference was for a quite different musical form for the celebration. They opted for singing in the vernacular, for musical forms in which everybody, both choir and congregation, could take an active part, and for a style in which both young and old would feel themselves at home.

With this the row began, and I was called on to mediate as an intermediary. The diagnosis was quickly made: the well-known tension between altar and choir-loft. The remedy? Only when people were ready to listen to each other, only when both parties were prepared for give and take, only then could one reach a compromise acceptable to both parties and a joint celebration could be held.

Conclusion

After twenty-five years all we can do is establish the fact that at all levels of the Church we have not yet found the balance between the demands made by the liturgy and the aspirations cherished by church music. 'What the Second Vatican Council did to the liturgy'—and, one can add, to music in the liturgy—'contains the seeds of a revolution the bearing of which only future generations will be able to gauge.'[8] A quarter of a century later that statement by J. Gelineau seems even more prophetic than when it was made.

Translated by Robert Nowell

Notes

1. I used the same title for my doctoral dissertation, G. Kock, *Tussen altaar en oksaal. Stromingen in de kerkmuziek na Vaticanum II*, MS doctoral thesis for the theological faculty, Tilburg, 1980.
2. E. Quack, '"Musik und Altar" und die liturgisch-kirchenmusikalische Reform', in *Musik und Altar*, 24 (1972), p. 148.
3. Quoted from P. Harnoncourt, *Die Kirchenmusik und das II Vatikanische Konzil* (papers of the Graz Church music week) (Graz 1965), p. 55.
4. J. Jungmann in *Commentary on the Documents of Vatican II*, ed. Herbert Vorgrimler (London/New York 1967), pp. 76–77.
5. H. Rennings, 'Die Instruktion über Gesang und Musik im Gottesdienst vom Jahre 1967', in *Liturgisches Jahrbuch* 17 (1967) 3, pp. 161–162.
6. H. Angles, commentary in *Musicae sacrae ministerium* 6 (1967), nos. 2–3, p. 37.
7. Paul VI, address to members of the Council for the Implementation of the Constitution on the Liturgy, 13 October 1966, *Katholiek Archief* 22 (1967), no. 5, col. 119.
8. J. Gelineau, 'Die Reform der Liturgie', in *Wort und Wahrheit* 19 (1964), quoted from H. Hucke, 'Church music', in *Concilium*, vol. 2, no. 1, February 1965, pp. 57–68.

Peter Jeffery

Chant East and West: Toward a Renewal of the Tradition

A holy and universal art

IN HIS *motu proprio 'Tra le sollecitudini'* (1903), often described as the charter of the liturgical movement, Pope Pius X called Gregorian chant 'the supreme model of church music,' so that 'the more a musical composition for the church approaches Gregorian melody in movement, inspiration, and taste, the more holy and the more liturgical it is' (TS, n. 3). In this he was building on the view that had been traditional since the middle ages: because the chant is 'inherited from the ancient Fathers' (TS, n. 3) and free of lascivious elements, it is superior to the newer styles of music that have developed in more recent times. The Eastern Orthodox churches have traditionally taken a similar position,[1] although polyphony is now common in the Byzantine Slavonic Mass. The Protestant Reformers had little use for medieval chant, but they recognised the value of some of its features. Calvin's ideal music, described in his preface to the Geneva Psalter (1543), had scriptural texts, set to unharmonised melodies, that were free of vain or sinful traits.

But *Tra le sollecitudini* was intended to go beyond what had been said in the past about the antiquity and moral goodness of the chant, to spell out clearly the principles regulating all sacred music. 'As its principal duty is to clothe the liturgical text ... with suitable melody,' we read, it must possess 'on the highest level' the three qualities that typify the liturgy itself: (1) holiness, (2) 'goodness of form' giving it the character of 'true art,' and (3) universality (TS, n. 2). It is because 'these qualities are found in the highest degree in Gregorian chant' (TS, n. 3), that it takes precedence over other kinds of music.

Because it outlined the nature of liturgical music in greater detail than any previous ecclesiastical document, and because it was among the very first papal statements imbued with the spirit of liturgical renewal, *Tra le sollecitudini* has served as the basis for much of the subsequent reflection on liturgical music among Catholics. This has of course led to further refinements, notably in the understanding of the attribute of holiness. The traditional negative explanation that emphasised the exclusion of secular elements was superseded when, in *Musicae Sacrae Disciplina* (1955), Pope Pius XII located the holiness of the chant in 'the close adaptation of the melody to the sacred text' of the liturgy, so that it is 'most intimately conformed to the words,' and 'interprets their force and efficacy' (MSD, n. 43). At Vatican II, *Sacrosanctum Concilium* brought words and music even closer together, and put both in the context of liturgical action. 'The musical tradition of the universal Church is a treasure of inestimable value, greater even than that of any other art. The main reason for this pre-eminence is that, as a combination of sacred music and words, it forms a necessary or integral part of the solemn liturgy. . . . Therefore sacred music is to be considered the more holy, the more closely connected it is with the liturgical action' (SC, n. 112).

In another area, that of universality, we have also moved beyond the view of Pius X, if only to the extent of being more sensitive to the complexity of the problem. His ideal now seems unrealistic in our pluralistic world: 'although every nation may be permitted to admit in its church compositions those special forms that may be said to constitute the specific character of its native music, these forms must be subordinated to the general characteristics of sacred music, in such a way that no person of another nation, upon hearing it, will experience any impression that is not good' (TS, n. 2). Pius XII, more aware of the great variety of cultures in the world, proposed that Gregorian chant itself could be a means of promoting universality. If it were sung 'in Catholic churches throughout the entire world,' then 'the faithful, wherever they may be, will hear music that is familiar to them,' and 'the unity and universality of the Church [will] shine forth more powerfully every day' (MSD, nn. 45–46).

But even within the Church, Pius XII had to admit that Gregorian chant was not exactly a universal: 'What We have said briefly here about Gregorian chant . . . can also, however, be applied to a certain extent to the liturgical chants of other rites—either to those of the West, such as the Ambrosian, Gallican or Mozarabic, or to the various Eastern rites. For as all of these display . . . the marvellous abundance of the Church, they also,

in their various liturgical chants, preserve treasures which must be guarded
...' (MSD, nn. 50–51). At Vatican II, no attempt was made to speak any
longer of universality in music. Gregorian chant was recognised as
'especially suited to the Roman liturgy' (SC, n. 116) while other musical
traditions, 'especially in mission lands' were to be 'held in proper esteem'
and given 'a suitable place' in worship (SC, n. 119). Even the Roman rite
was no longer regarded as nigh universal, but as equal to the eastern rites
(*Orientalium Ecclesiarum*, n. 3).

As for 'goodness of form,' the Council described the entire 'musical
tradition of the universal Church,' and not chant only or primarily, as a
'treasure of inestimable value' (SC, n. 112). It 'approves all forms of true
art ... so long as they accord with the spirit of liturgical action' (SC,
n. 116). Therefore it was decreed that 'the treasury of sacred music is to be
preserved and cultivated with great care' (SC, n. 114), while congregational
singing, in both Latin and the vernacular, was also to be fostered (SC,
nn. 30, 54, 113–114, 118).

This twofold mandate was imperfectly carried out after the Council,
because of a split that rapidly developed among church musicians. Many
musicians trained in classical art music, who cared most about preserving
the sacred treasury, were accused of trying to discourage congregational
singing. Those most committed to congregational singing, many of whom
promoted the use of music composed in 'folk' (or, more accurately,
popular) style, were accused of trying to banish the treasury altogether
from liturgical use. The polarisation began immediately after the Council
and has remained,[2] the views of the two camps summed up in the titles of
the North American periodicals *Sacred Music* and *Pastoral Music*.

One unfortunate result of this polarisation has been to postpone what
should have been an immediate response to the Council's directives, namely
the objective reassessment of the chant in the new light of liturgical renewal,
parallelling the reflection and renewal fostered by the Council in other areas
of the Church's life. Instead, much of what has been written on chant and
liturgical music since the Council has, sadly, been aimed mainly at
defending the one-sided views of either the 'sacred' or the 'pastoral' group.
Much that was tendentious and ill-considered—even ill-informed—found
its way into publication, the bulk of it written by performing musicians
with limited academic training in the historical, sociological, and
anthropological study of music, who were scarcely equipped to investigate
the new questions being raised about the pastoral functions music should
serve in community worship.

No one would write about any other theological subject without being
fully informed of current scholarship in all the relevant fields. Writing on

liturgical music must be informed by musical scholarship, in addition to theology and musical practice, because it is the critical study of the primary sources that has animated the modern renewal in every area of the life of the Church. Besides biblical and patristic studies, which shed indirect light on the earliest Christian music that does not actually survive, the two indispensable scholarly fields are: (1) the historical study of the medieval eastern and western chant repertories, which crystallised the traditions of early Christian music just as the great sacramentaries codified the heritage of early Christian prayer, and (2) the anthropological study of the broad human experience of religious music.

The inclusion of the eastern church and non-Christian religions helps correct the inevitable distortions that arise from exclusive reliance on western Christian primary sources. The cross-cultural approach puts the tension between 'sacred' and 'pastoral' music in perspective, for both approaches originated within western Christianity and are rare outside it. This article can only point out a few areas where a new return to the primary sources can lead to a new consensus, fairer to Christian history and more faithful to the directives of the Council.

2. Three areas for re-examination

(a) Holy texts and their melodies

Since the Council, the close relationship between the Gregorian chant melodies and their Latin texts has often been said to disqualify them for use in vernacular liturgical celebration. This belief, common among both 'sacred' and 'pastoral' musicians, has discouraged attemps both to perform Latin chant in otherwise vernacular liturgies, and to adapt the melodies to vernacular translations of the texts. But the known evidence does not justify rigid positions on such questions. It is anachronistic, for instance, to suppose that each individual chant melody was especially composed to fit the specific text with which we find it.

Recent chant scholarship has called new attention to the 'formulaic' character of many of the melodies, which are constructed from stereotyped phrases and 'melody types' that are highly flexible, and have been re-used again and again with many different texts. Similar phenomena have been observed in other cultures that lack written music notation—they seem to result from one way the human memory stores large repertories of melodies. In the medieval Christian chant traditions, then, it is apparently a relic of the time before the invention of the neumes (ninth to tenth centuries), when the vast corpus of melodies could only be preserved by memory.[3] The possibility that such formulas could be adapted creatively to texts in modern languages is certainly not to be excluded *a priori*; medieval singers themselves did not shrink from translating chant texts. Translations from Greek are found in all the western and eastern chant repertories. Beginning in the ninth century the entire corpus of Byzantine chant was translated into Slavonic, with great care taken to preserve the original Greek meters and melodies as much as possible.

Opponents of translating Gregorian chant often claim that the phonetics of modern vernacular languages distort the medieval melodies, which were conceived with Latin phonemics in mind. But this is the way the melodies were sung for centuries—since at least the late middle ages liturgical Latin has been pronounced everywhere according to the rules of the local vernacular. The so-called Roman pronunciation of Latin, with its pure italianate vowels, became normative only in our own century. No one knows how Latin was pronounced in the time and place (or more probably the several times and places) in which the chant was created, for the question of when and where Gregorian chant originated is the most hotly debated issue in medieval musicology.

Much the same problem troubles the claim that the medieval melodies are specially molded to the patterns of Latin accentuation, so that something is lost when they are reset to languages with different accentuation rules. Actually there is no scholarly agreement as to how the Latin accents may be reflected in the Gregorian melodies.[4] Renaissance humanists found the melodies so deficient in this regard that they thoroughly revised them, producing the truncated and altered melodies that ultimately appeared in the infamous Ratisbon editions of the late nineteenth century.

Only to a limited degree do the chant melodies seem to respond to the semantics of the text through word-painting and similar devices. It is when we come to syntax that we can detect a consistent relationship betwen the words and the music. 'In effect, a chant melody records a reading of its text; the melody is the record of its maker's responses to the relationships among word order, syntax, and phrasing and to the ways these are related to the text's meaning. . . . In this process, melody plays a role similar to that of punctuation' by clearly marking off syntactical units.[5] This is consistent with the probable historical origin of the chant in such practices as psalmodic recitation and biblical cantillation, in both of which the melody is shaped mainly by the syntax of the text.

Accordingly, sensitive, creative adaptations of the chant melodies to modern languages may indeed be possible, because the syntactical structure of the psalms and other chant texts can often be translated effectively from one language to another. This is evident in the many new psalm tones by modern composers, which, though intended for vernacular psalmody, often resemble the medieval psalm tones in melodic shape, being composed of a few repeated phrases, each consisting of a reciting tone interrupted by inflections or cadences.

The structural similarity of the chant melodies to cantillation, the solemn melodious proclamation of sacred texts, is a reminder that listening, like performing, is a legitimate musical activity. In our time, when so much effort has been needed to foster congregational singing, this truth is often overlooked or even denied. But the experience of hearing the Word of God and the prayer of the Church (*Dei Verbum*, nn. 1, 21) is only intensified when these texts are sung. 'Sweetness of melody mixed with doctrine' ensures that we 'absorb . . . the words through . . . ease of hearing' (St Basil, PG 29, 212). Even when words are lacking or in an unknown tongue, the music itself can mediate certain types of religious experience, for music communicates something which cannot easily be put into words (SC, n. 120). This is why the act of listening to music has often been treated as a metaphor for contemplation,[6] because 'the strong connection of music with religion' in all cultures 'draws us to the conclusion that one of the main functions of music for man is communication with the supernatural'.[7] The real problem is that Catholics have not yet learned to achieve a reasonable balance between congregational singing and active listening, a balance that existed in parts of the early church and that Protestant congregations maintain today.

(b) *True art or virtuosity*

The polarisation among musicians has often taken the form of confrontation over artistic quality. Some 'sacred' musicians, quick to decry the superficiality and amateurish performances of so much 'Folk Mass' music, succeed only in confirming the suspicions of some 'pastoral' musicians, who seem to feel that classical music and chant are elitist and inaccessible to the modern churchgoer. Against such patronising attitudes toward the faithful, the Council emphasised the Christian duty 'to make all persons aware of their right to culture' (*Gaudium et Spes*, n. 60). The value of classical music for pastoral worship is demonstrated regularly in Protestant churches, where hymns and choir music by the best composers in western history handsomely support full participation by all the people in musical pastoral worship.

The charge that Gregorian chant is elitist has even been given a pseudo-historical foundation. Because much of the authentic repertoire is too difficult for modern congregations to sing, many have supposed that the chant as we know it was actually created by elite medieval soloists who, to show off their own musical virtuosity, destroyed the original Christian tradition of congregational song by embellishing the (allegedly) simple, folk-like melodies inherited from the early church. Versions of this claim have been disseminated by many writers, but supporting evidence is scarce. No critical history of early Christian performance practice has ever been written, but there are enough references to soloists and choirs in early Christian writings to quash allegations that singing was exclusively congregational until it was expropriated by specialists. Scholars are only beginning to unravel the diversity of musical practices that are often mentioned but hardly ever carefully explained in the literature of the early church.

The idea that the florid Gregorian melodies developed from simpler originals through a process of gradual ornamentation has some support among chant scholars, but at present it remains a theory that cannot actually be demonstrated. If such a process actually took place, however, we cannot merely assume that it began because highly trained virtuosi were eager to display their talents, or that it necessarily displaced congregational singing. In many cultures scholars have observed that traditional ceremonial melodies, handed on orally over many centuries, become increasingly slower in tempo and (as if to compensate) more heavily ornamented. But this happens whether or not the performers are skilled specialists; it may be no more than a very human process of respectful remembering.

Nor is congregational singing necessarily hindered. In certain very conservative Protestant communities, which never made use of virtuoso professionals, simple hymn tunes that have become extremely elaborate are still performed by the whole congregation.[8] Thus, as we have no idea what early Christian congregations were or were not capable of, there is no basis for claiming that their melodies must have been simple, or that the prolix melodies of medieval chant represent a departure from their original state. The decline of congregational song in the late patristic period probably had more to do with sociological factors, especially the clericalisation and monasticisation of the liturgy. Particularly interesting is the case of Byzantine chant, where a steadily advancing process of melodic elaboration, indeed the work of highly skilled musical specialists, was active from at least the ninth century down to the present. Yet the singing of the people seems to have begun to decline well before then—it may have been more an indirect cause of the ornamentation process than a direct result of it.

The high artistic value of Gregorian chant is still evident today to many westerners (though indeed not to all), even to some with little musical education, and even to some of the young and the un-churched who have no nostalgia for the pre-conciliar Roman liturgy they never experienced. To many who know no Latin, the chant still conveys a strong feeling of elevated spirituality, at a time when so many other cultural vestiges of Christendom have lost their meaning for people attracted by new cults, eastern religions, anti-historical fundamentalism, even apathetic agnosticism. Chant recordings continue to sell, and jazz and rock musicians have occasionally based new music on Gregorian themes recalled from childhood.[9] No one can receive a university or conservatory degree in music without some exposure to chant, and to teach music history at a secular university is to be asked every term, by people of all and no religious persuasions, why the Church abandoned such an extraordinary artistic treasure. Certainly the potential still exists for using the chant to promote 'a higher understanding of truth, goodness, and beauty,' by which many people 'can be more easily drawn to the worship and contemplation of the creator' (*Gaudium et Spes*, n. 57). Wider familiarity with chant could only raise artistic standards for all the other music used in the liturgy (SC, nn. 121–122, 124), emphasising solid, stable values over ephemeral trendiness. The challenge is to find ways of creatively, effectively using the chant to achieve the overall goals of cultural pluralism and pastoral worship.

(c) Universality in music and worship

'Sacred' musicians have been known to argue that classical art music possesses an intrinsically sacred character, more appropriate for worship than 'folk' (*i.e.* popular) music, which is typically preoccupied with such secular concerns as erotic love, vain showmanship, even drug abuse. 'Pastoral' musicians, inspired by the Council's new openness to all the cultures of the world, have sometimes replied that no musical style is inherently sacred or secular, that the very idea of an intrinsically sacred music is a relatively recent European development, that the music of almost any culture can be adapted to liturgical purposes. In fact, however, both arguments are unfounded and self-defeating. In classical music, from Palestrina to Mozart, the distinction between sacred and secular styles was often less sharp in practice than it is sometimes said to have been in theory. The very idea of distinguishing the two is neither new nor particularly European; some non-western cultures separate them more rigidly, even to the point of having no common word for 'music' that can denote both.[10] On the other hand, the twin concepts of 'art music' and 'folk music' primarily reflect the outlook of the West, where they have historically strong emotional connotations that cripple the present liturgical debate because they are unrecognised by either side. Finally, those who claim to respect cultural diversity cannot reasonably argue that European concepts of sacred music are less worthy of inculturation and renewal than the traditions of non-western countries.

The entire complex of issues falls within what ethnomusicologists call the question of 'musical universals.' Are there any musical characteristics that are recognised by all or most of the human race as particularly suitable for music to be used in worship? Unfortunately we cannot even begin to answer questions like these, partly because there are far too many cultures about which we lack even basic data, partly because it is so difficult even to frame such questions in ways that every culture would find intelligible. However, people of many religions do worship with music that has important similarities to Christian liturgical chant. Monophonic vocal melodies with little or no harmonisation or instrumental accompaniment, making use of elastic melody-types and short stereotyped phrases, are set to words derived from religious scriptures, in ways that especially emphasise the syntactical divisions of the text—this description could with few adjustments fit the liturgical chant of Jews, Muslims, Hindus, and some Buddhists as well as that of eastern and western Christians.[11] To consider these features typical of liturgical music is, then, to be in agreement with a large portion of humanity (cf. Nostra Aetate, n. 2).

Both the 'sacred' and 'pastoral' outlooks have been overly narrow. True universality—which is to say Catholicism—will come neither through enforced uniformity nor shallow broad-mindedness. It will come when everything of value, whether from the storehouse of the past or the bazaar of the present, 'contributes its own gifts to other parts and to the whole Church, so that the whole and each of the parts are strengthened by the common sharing' (Lumen Gentium, n. 13). To bring this about will require discernment, informed by critical study of the primary sources with open minds and charitable hearts. But the renewal of liturgical music will only be possible when the theological and pastoral discussion is held to the same high critical standard as in liturgical renewal generally. Then the Church, like the householder who brings forth from his treasury both new and old (Matt. 13:52), will have begun to recover the authentic tradition of liturgical music, centered on the hearing and singing of the Holy Word in fitting melody, 'seeking the noble beauty' of 'truly sacred art' (SC, n. 124), in harmony with—but also redeeming—the universal musical and relgious experience of the entire human race.

Notes

1. See D. Stefanovic, 'Die orthodoxe Kirche', *Religiöse Autoritäten und Musik: Ein Symposium*, ed. D. Baumann and K. Von Fischer (Kassel 1984), p. 89.

2. See *Sacred Music and Liturgy Reform after Vatican II: Proceedings of the Fifth International Church Music Congress, Chicago-Milwaukee, August 21–28, 1966*, ed. J. Overath (Rome 1969), pp. 108–110, 284–288. M. T. Winter, *Why Sing? Toward a Theology of Catholic Church Music* (Washington DC 1984), pp. 3–27.

3. 'Transmission and Form in Oral Traditions', *International Musicological Society: Report of the Twelfth Congress, Berkeley 1977*, ed. D. Heartz and B. Wade (Kassel 1981), pp. 139–211.

4. For three quite different views see: W. Apel, *Gregorian Chant* (Bloomington, Indiana 1958), pp. 275–304; J. Stevens, *Words and Music in the Middle Ages: Song, Narrative, Dance and Drama, 1050–1350* (Cambridge 1986), pp. 277–283; J. Viret, *Le chant grégorien, musique de la parole sacrée* (Lausanne 1986), pp. 139–165.

5. R. Jonsson and L. Treitler, 'Medieval Music and Language: A Reconsideration of the Relationship', *Music and Language*, (Studies in the History of Music 1) (New York 1983), p. 22.

6. J. Prou, 'Gregorian Chant in the Spirituality of the Church', *Gregorian Chant in Liturgy and Education: An International Symposium, June 19–22, 1983* (Washington DC 1983), pp. 25–38. See also R. Otto, *The Idea of the Holy*, transl. J. W. Harvey (New York 1958), pp. 47 49, 68–71 (*Das Heilige*, Sonderausgabe, München 1963, pp. 63–65, 89–91.

7. B. Nettl, 'The Role of Music in Culture: Iran, A Recently Developed Nation', *Contemporary Music and Music Cultures*, ed. C. Hamm *et al.* (Englewood Cliffs, New Jersey 1975), p. 98.

8. N. Temperley, 'The Old Way of Singing: Its Origins and Development', *Journal of the American Musicological Society* (1981), pp. 511–544.

9. See A. Broadbent's 'Tantum ergo: In Memoriam—Edward Kennedy Ellington' recorded on: Woody Herman and the Thundering Herd, *Herd at Montreaux*, Fantasy Records F-9470, 1974. Even the rock musician Frank Zappa, whose name is virtually synonymous with irreverence and iconoclasm, recently told an interviewer, 'I've always liked the sound of Gregorian chants . . . I've wound up playing it on the guitar in the middle of solos . . .'. P. Occhiogrosso, *Once a Catholic* (Boston 1987), p. 338.

10. An introduction to this and other problems is T. Ellingson, 'Music and Religion', *The Encyclopedia of Religion* (New York 1987), 10:163–172.

11. J. Spector, 'Chanting', *Encyclopedia of Religion* 3:204–213. See also: 'Mediterranean Studies: Chant Traditions and Liturgy', in *International Musicological Society: Report*, 402–435.

Lawrence A. Hoffman

Musical Traditions and Tensions in the American Synagogue

Speaking of music

IT IS difficult to know how to speak of music within the context of Jewish worship. Not that it was always so:[1] from the earliest of times, music and prayer were seen in complementary fashion: a veritable orchestra in the Temple, a sacrificial cult inseparable from the Levitical choir, and antiphonal psalmody in both Temple and nascent synagogue. Rabbinic pronouncements from the same period, but extending also throughout the Middle Ages, similarly link liturgy to musical performance, to the extent that, from time to time, we even get an inkling of a theology of liturgical music presupposed by the speakers. Some texts actually express that theology in some detail: mystical midrashim (c. third to eighth centuries) liken Israel's worship to the angelic heavenly choir, for example, structuring human praise of God after the responsive pattern presumed from a juxtaposition of Isaiah 6:3 and Ezekiel 3:12; Kabbalists developed musical societies to welcome the Sabbath, while individual theorists, like Abraham Abulafia (1240–1291) combined musical instruction with the liturgical recitation of the letters in the divine name, in order to induce an ecstatic trance.[2] It might even be argued that despite considerable Jewish iconography, Jews were not given sufficient freedom to achieve the visual artistry that one finds in cathedral or mosque; so they coded their culture, not in frescoes, statuary and arches, but in *music*—even Talmudic *study* was accompanied by recitation melodies. Yet, to return to my point of departure, in contrast to the considerable literature available on other liturgical issues (like history of texts, and prayer book reform), the role of music in contemporary worship is practically unresearched and undiscussed.

In part, we are victims of an unfortunate logocentrism going back at least to the founders of the *Wissenschaft* tradition, men like Leopold Zunz (1794–1886) and Ismar Elbogen (1874–1943) who established the canons of modern Jewish liturgical scholarship. They catalogued poetry, traced prayer recension, and mapped prayer rites, without, however, giving much thought to worship as performative. Rooted in Germany's academic philological tradition, they understood liturgy as purely a matter of sorting through manuscripts with a view toward unpacking the history of the texts that constitute the prayer corpus.[3] They (and their academic successors) do mention music on occasion; and they treat the role of the prayer leader and the congregation; but they do so only to reconstitute the history of the intergenerational *text* of prayer from its origins in antiquity to their own time.[4]

Uneasiness about music was actually part of a long-standing rabbinic bias typical of northern and eastern Europe beginning in the twelfth century, but particularly evident during the rise of the professional cantorate there from the seventeenth century onward. The fact is that Jewish tradition has always been ambivalent about music, favouring it as angelic in essence and the only proper way to reach the Creator, but fearing it also, an attitude going back, possibly, to the rabbinic reservations about music's centrality in pagan rituals.[5] Whatever its origin, this latent suspicion of music as unseemly, and perhaps even demonic, underlies many rabbinic dicta that are repeated through the ages. General music-making was officially banned, either because Jews should mourn the Temple's destruction; or because of music's inherent sensuality; or because some musical forms seem to ape non-Jewish custom.[6] Were worship not a religious obligation, even liturgical music might have been banned; as it was, its licit parameters were always being questioned.

This ambiguity about music is traceable particularly to the twelfth/thirteenth century German pietistic tradition called *Hasidei Ashkenaz*, founded by Samuel HeHasid (c. twelfth century) and his son Judah (c. 1150–1217). These pietists saw prayer as humanity's highest task, and understood it to require music, in that only music can divert one's mind from pedestrian concerns, and shape instead the thought complex suggested by each word of the liturgical text. The result was a genuine cantorial tradition where music was primary. But even for them, music served text, not the other way around, and there is reason to suspect a growing antagonism between the musical class of cantors and their textual masters, the rabbis. Judah, for example, objects to collecting donations from wedding guests to pay the cantor's fee. The issue did not go away. The Polish authority, Samuel Edels (1555–1631) agrees, on the grounds that people are cajoled into paying the cantor, so that 'this is a case of robbery, not gift-giving'. Apparently, the demand for music at religious events ranging from the daily liturgy to weddings made the cantor a necessity. But concern over the cantorial art as suspect prevented the same cantor from being accorded emoluments and status indicative of high regard.

By the seventeenth century, we find the institutionalisation of the cantor as a sociologically marginal personality, in whom society projected characteristics of both horns of its dilemma. Officially, cantors were necessary; but unofficially, they were deemed untrustworthy, and even portrayed proverbially as fools; that is, as musical, but not textual, savants. As communities grew in size, particularly under the continued influence of the mystical tradition in which prayer had particular significance, increased attention was paid to the communal liturgy and its accompanying music. Handbooks offering advice to cantors demonstrate the conflict at its height. Some of the cantors were themselves rabbis, of course, but in the main, we find non-cantorial rabbinic authorities excoriating non-rabbinic cantorial artists for caring only about vocal performance, garbling textual grammar or syntax, and going so far as to spend 'one-quarter of an hour in the vocalisation of a silent letter!'[7] That these rabbinic critics were as expert with words as the cantors were with song resulted in some rather one-sided trenchant remarks, which posterity retained. Thus music was recognised as angelic and demonic, both; so that musicians who sang it were cast in the unenviable and ambivalent role of saint and sinner.

The point is that a straight line leads from the pietistic consciousness of twelfth century Germany to the scholars who formulated modern liturgical study. By definition, the written text was deserving of study, whereas the musical means by which it was presented was not. Discussion of music has remained almost exclusively the domain of musicians, largely the cantors and composers in and for the synagogue. But there has been no dialogue with the rabbis, who today, usually go merrily about their own business discussing theology, liturgy and prayer, as if musical considerations were mere window-dressing to be applied later by a staff of musically competent technicians. Even seminary training has, until recently, trained cantors as singers, but withheld from their education the theological perspective deemed necessary for rabbis. If we are to speak intelligently of worship and music as a single entity, we will have to do more than simply summarise what has been said thus far. We will have to start all over again.

This article seeks to do just that: to provide a theological perspective that frames the problems faced by the contemporary synagogue as it considers the role of music. This new perspective must (a) be true to Jewish categories of understanding; (b) explain the state of affairs evident to observers of Jewish worship today; and (c) draw authentically on the musical heritage with which it claims to be continuous.

I turn first to (c), the synagogue musical heritage, where I will contrast traditional music with art music, and both of these (which are elitist) with contemporary populism. With the help of some sociological theory on the nature of artistic disputes, we will then turn to a fresh look at (b), the empirical evidence of our time. Finally, I suggest the outlines of a solution, in line with (a): Jewish ecclesiology.

The Music of the Synagogue

The variety of music Jews have called sacred is quite remarkable!

(1) The ancient Temple featured Levitical choirs and accompanying instrumentation that included woodwinds, percussion, brass and strings.

(2) Synagogue music (by the twelfth century) varied, but included (for example): (*a*) responsorial psalmody, between prayer leader and congregation, going back to the Mishnaic period; (*b*) biblical chant, first, according to hand signs (chironomy) and, eventually, following accent marks accompanying the canonised text, as it was fixed in tenth-century Palestine; (*c*) prayer modes linked to calendrical occasions, known (singly) as *nusach*: that is, discrete sets of musical motives which undergo constant improvisation: (*d*) popular melodies borrowed from the culture at large, or evolved by the folk.

(3) By the twelfth century, local musico-liturgical traditions were crystallising, the northern European (or Ashkenazic) variety, for example, usually ascribed to Jacob Moellin (the Maharil: 1360?–1427), who is said to have transmitted melodies *Misinai* ('from Mt Sinai), these being the oldest clearly recognisable liturgical motives, datable, at most, a century or two earlier.

(4) In the nineteenth century, music moved in one of two directions. 'Traditionalistic' congregations featured worship in the inherited pre-modern Hebrew text rendered in a style unconcerned with 'modern' aesthetics. There, particularly in eastern Europe where Kabbalistic theories of music and prayer predominated, Jews elaborated upon an already-present cantorial solo mode. The cantor, or *chazzan*, specialised in a finely-crafted and intricately executed recitative filled with melismatic passages that were rooted in the *nusach*. People who speak of Jewish liturgical music, usually mean this specialised cantorial style.

(5) An alternative route was the equivalent of a Jewish Reformation, which differed, musically speaking, from the Christian parallel, in that Judaism had no strong unison singing tradition among its clerics, so never developed the parallel phenomenon, congregational hymns, among its laity. (In fact, despite official hymnals issued off and on since 1897, and as recently as 1987, the American Reform Movement's attempt to introduce hymn singing has consistently failed.[8]) Instead, Reform Judaism mutated the art form that it did have, namely, the cantorial solo. Jews, who had newly received civil rights on condition that they act 'civilly', thus refurbished old synagogue favorites, which emerged no longer in pure modal form, but instead, suitably harmonised through the imposition of a tonal system, and firmly notated beyond the possibility of free cantorial elaboration; and they discovered art music, newly composed for performance by soloists, who were often great voices hired to replace the cantor, whose expertise in Jewish musical tradition was deemed unimportant. (The closest historical precedent to the new art form was the work of Salamone de Rossi, a seventeenth-century Mantuan composer whose style typified the high Renaissance court.)

(6) The music of Jewish reform took shape under Cantor Solomon Sulzer (1804–1890) in Vienna, and then moved westward toward the urban capitals of enlightenment culture like Berlin and Hamburg. In Poland, meanwhile, Hasidic Judaism developed wordless melodies called *niggunim*, rooted in native—and not necessarily Jewish—folk tunes.

(7) Finally, we have the influence of our own age, in which most of the strands mentioned above have their devotees. Art-music vies with trendy folk singing, sung alongside a modified *niggun*, chanted psalms, the ubiquitous presence of summer-camp and youth music, and rediscovered *nusach* too—rendered by cantors who once more are in demand. There are surprises here too: secular—even nationalistic—favourites from Israel, expressing no prayer book wording at all, but singing of Jerusalem or of Jewish aspirations in a post-Holocaust age. One even hears services concluding with *Hatikvah*, the national anthem of the State of Israel, clearly dependent on *The Moldau* for its melody, but expressing in its lyrics 'the hope of 2000 years, to be a free people in our land, the land of Zion and Jerusalem'—lyrics taken as sacred by Jews in our time. Especially in America, the state of liturgical music is best characterised as open, changeable, and democratic—maybe even chaotic.

Thus, the problem: given this rich heritage, and the contemporary fluidity, what are appropriate guidelines in the search for the music of Jewish prayer? The problem is both musical and social.

The situation today

Musically, two separate, but interlinked, issues should not be confused. The nineteenth century's division into what I have called 'traditionalistic' and 'Reform' resulted at first in a simple conflict between the traditional cantorial music as it had evolved by then, and the burgeoning art music borrowed from the environment. By and large, the American Reform Movement and its liberal European counterparts institutionalised the latter option; the Orthodox and Conservative Movements retained the former. But both options were alike in that they were equally elitist, the only question being which elite was selected as worthy of emulation: the arcane world of cantorial *nusach*, or the aristocratic taste of upper-class Europe. Within the last several decades, a new conflict has emerged: a challenge to elitism *per se*. Worship is seen more and more as belonging to the people, and demanding, therefore, an engaging musical style that evokes their active participation. By contrast, both cantorial music and art music are incomprehensible to all but very sophisticated worshippers. From the perspective of the cantor, the demand for musical 'accessibility' threatens both the age-old internally authentic tradition and the relatively new externally authentic art-music tradition too, since the newest sing-along tunes may lack roots in the synagogue's history and fail the test of refined taste as well.

But here the social dynamic becomes painfully evident. We saw above how cantors were carefully excluded from positions of authority, while rabbis ignored music in favour of text. Thus in today's synagogue, cantorial demands for musical authenticity are often met by rabbis who claim that artistic excellence may be counter-productive to the goal of communal worship in a democratic age. The sociology of art is helpful here. Herbert Gans studied cultural disputes revolving about 'popular culture and high culture', and concluded that the ideological critiques of the former by advocates of the latter mask the fact that at issue is a relative loss of stature by the elite, who thus constitute 'downwardly mobile groups [who] exaggerate their own loss of influence into a theory of overall social deterioration . . . [and erect] an ideology of defense, constructed to protect the cultural and political privileges of high culture'.[9] High culture, he says, is 'creator-oriented' in that it serves the aesthetic needs of its creators; popular culture is 'user-oriented' in that it seeks justification for its existence among the people who use it.

Clearly this characterisation describes our situation, though it raises more problems than it solves. Whether cantors traditionally were downwardly mobile is questionable, but they were already low in status (as we saw), and if we do not have extant their own spirited defence of their art, that can only be because the rabbis controlled the written canon of what got transmitted to us. Since the nineteenth century, however, power has clearly moved away from its traditional seat among those knowledgable in tradition, and cantors are certainly among these. But rampant democracy of values has also unseated the cultural elite of Europe, so that even the proponents of art music are on the defensive. The dominant conflict over the popularisation of liturgical experience mirrors the social conflict in which the worshipping masses can opt out of worship altogether if they dislike what happens there, so that rabbis charged with prayer do what they can to make sure that, within appropriate bounds, the people will in fact like it.

Towards a solution

Clearly, even the rabbis charged with bringing in the sheep are not seriously discussing pandering to the masses without regard for theological considerations. But what should those considerations be? Even a valid reduction of the problem to its sociological reality is still a reduction to a level at which religion refuses to operate. How, then, does Jewish ecclesiology provide at least the framework in which a solution will be found?

The answer lies in the very essence of the cantorial role as defined from its inception. We saw that the synagogue service was designed essentially as an antiphonal interaction between the congregation and its elected prayer-leader, known in Hebrew as the *sheliach tzibbur*, literally, 'the agent of the congregation', who is charged with singing the liturgy on the people's behalf. This was a conscious emulation of the angelic bands said to be alternating in their praise of God.

The best analogy I can think of is classical social contract theory, under which it is assumed that sovereign individuals in a presumed state of nature once gave up rights to a monarch, in order to further interests which could not be achieved in the state of nature itself. So too, although individuals in the state of nature can worship God, Jews opted at Sinai to exchange that state of nature for the covenant, the fulfilment of which demanded abrogation of rampant individualism and vesting certain leaders with unique prerogatives. The cantor as 'agent of the congregation' thus emerged as that person who is given the special duty and right to plead on the people's behalf before God.

The philosophical issue for social contract political thought is the determination of a proper balance between the powers of the ruler and the inalienable rights still inherent in the people. That precisely is the issue in debate here: to what extent may the people invoke their own taste in worship, as their inalienable right before the true Ruler of rulers? To what extent can the *sheliach tzibbur* claim an obligation to the traditional norms of the covenant which the people entered once for all time? The parallels between *sheliach tzibbur* and the ruler in social contract theory go deep: the praying congregation must contain a quorum of at least ten worshippers, symbolic of the communal base for Jewish prayer; the liturgy even contains a ritualised statement in which the cantor requests permission from the people to continue particularly complex poetry; and the Talmud—no less than John Locke!—discusses when a treacherous cantor as agent of the people can be removed by those whom he (nowadays, also she) represents.

Conclusion

It is too early to define solutions. We have yet to understand what a solution will look like. Hence, this paper, which describes the background to the 'miscommunication' between rabbi and cantor based on a deep-seated ambivalence to music's expressive power, puts forward an alternative and non-judgmental model that allows for conflict but is rooted in the social contract inherent to Jewish ecclesiology. Clearly, we have long passed the day when prayer leaders—rabbi or cantor—can presume to prescribe what is best without taking counsel with the laity. Certainly too, we have gone beyond the revolution of the '60's in which any old sing-along melody was taken up in reaction to the prior rule of the elite. As agents of the people in more ways than one, rabbis and cantors are now emerging as dialogue partners, both with each other and with the people they serve. Heard here and there is music built (perhaps) on *nusach* and set to traditional texts, often for solo cantorial voice, with, however, a responsive refrain and a readily identifiable melody line modified by simple but sophisticated harmony. That, I think, is the breakthrough toward which we are tending—a novel *nusach America*: an authentically Jewish and American sound encompassing traditionalism and art music, elitism and populism; a compromise consistent with the evolving synagogue and the divine service of our time.

Notes

1. For an excellent overview and bibliography, see Hanoch Avenary, 'Music' in *Encyclopedia Judaica* (Jerusalem 1972), Vol. 12, pp. 554–678.
2. See Moshe Idel, *The Mystical Experience in Abraham Abulafia* (Albany, N.Y. 1988), pp. 53–71.

3. For details, and suggestions for a novel approach to prayer as prayer, rather than as text, see Lawrence A. Hoffman, *Beyond the Text: a Holistic Approach to Liturgy* (Bloomington 1987).

4. See, for example, Elbogen's classic 'Studies in Jewish Liturgy' (1906: reprinted in Jakob J. Petuchowski, *Contributions to the Study of Jewish Liturgy*, New York 1970).

5. Eric Werner *The Sacred Bridge*, Vol. 2 (New York 1984), p. 23), calls it 'an age of anti-musical Puritanism'.

6. For traditional summary of views, see Rabbi Aharon Kahn, 'Music in Halachic Perspective', *Journal of Halacha and Contemporary Society* 14 (Fall, 1987), pp. 7–48.

7. See Stefan C. Relf, *Shabbethai Sofer and his Prayer-book* (Cambridge 1979), pp. 36–37; p. 93, n. 62.

8. For details, see Lawrence A. Hoffman, *Gates of Understanding*, Vol. 1 (New York 1977), pp. 27–35.

9. Herbert J. Gans, *Popular Culture and High Culture: an Analysis and Evaluation of Taste* (New York 1974), pp. 55–56, 63.

PART II

Music in Black African Traditions of Worship

James Cone

Black Spirituals: A Theological Interpretation

A LARGE amount of scholarship has been devoted to the music and poetry of the black spiritual but little has been written about its theology. Apparently most scholars assume that the value of the black spiritual lies in its artistic expression and not its theological content, which could be taken to mean that blacks can 'sing and dance good' but cannot think. For example almost everyone agrees with W. E. B. DuBois' contention that 'the Negro is primarily an artist'[1] and that his gift of music to America is unsurpassed. But what about the black person as a philosopher and theologian? Is it not possible that the thought of the spiritual is as profound as its music is creative, since without thought art is impossible? In this article, my purpose is to investigate the theological implications of the black spirituals, with special reference to the meaning of God, Jesus Christ, suffering and eschatology.

The birth of spirituals

No theological interpretation of the black spirituals is valid that ignores the cultural environment that created them, and understanding a culture means, in part, perceiving its history. Black history in America is a history of black servitude, a record of pain and sorrows, of slave ships, and auction blocks. It is the story of black life in chains and of what that meant for the souls and bodies of black people. This is the history that created the

41

spirituals, and it must be recognised if we are to render a valid theological interpretation of these black songs.

Physical slavery was cruel. It meant working fifteen to twenty hours per day and being beaten unmercifully if one displayed the slightest fatigue. The auction block became a symbol of 'brokenness' because no family ties were recognised. Husbands were separated from wives and children from parents. There were few laws protecting the slaves, since most whites believed that Africans were only partly human (three-fifths was the fraction fixed by the Founding Fathers in framing the constitution in 1787). Later, to put down any lingering doubts about black humanity, the highest court of the land decreed that black people had no rights which white people were bound to respect. Slaves were property, as were animals and objects; their owners could dispose of them as they saw fit—provided they did not endanger the welfare of the society as a whole.

But the history that created the spirituals contains much more than what white people *did* to black people. Black history is also the record of black people's historical strivings, an account of their perceptions of their existence in an oppressive society. What whites did to blacks is secondary. The primary reality is what blacks did to whites in order to restrict the white assault on their humanity.

When white people enslaved Africans, their intention was to dehistoricise black existence, to foreclose the possibility of a future defined by the African heritage. White people demeaned the sacred tales of the black ancestors, ridiculing their myths and defiling the scared rites. Their intention was to define humanity according to European definitions so that their brutality against Africans could be characterised as civilising the savages. But white Europeans did not succeed, and black history is the record of their failure. Black people did not stand by passively while white oppressors demoralised their being. Many rebelled—physically and mentally. Black history in America is the history of that rebellion.

To understand the history of black resistance, it is also necessary to know the black spirituals. They are historical songs which speak about the rupture of black lives; they tell us about a people in the land of bondage and what they did to hold themselves together and to fight back. We are told that the people of Israel could not sing the Lord's song in a strange land. But, for blacks, their *being* depended upon a song. Through song, they built new structures for a measure of African identity while living in the midst of American slavery, providing both the substance of the rhythm to cope with human servitude.

Much has been said about the compensatory and otherworldly ideas in the black spirituals. While I do not question the presence of that theme, there is, nevertheless another train of thought running through these songs. And unless this emphasis is considered, it is impossible for the spirituals to be correctly understood. I am referring to the emphasis on freedom in this world, and the kinds of risks blacks were willing to take in order to attain it.

> Oh Freedom! Oh Freedom!
> Oh Freedom, over me!
> An' befo' I'd be a slave,
> I'll be buried in my grave,
> An' go home to my Lord and be free.
> Didn't my Lord deliver Daniel,
> Deliver Daniel, deliver Daniel.
> An' why not a-every man?
> Why can't he deliver me?

The theme of freedom and activities it implied explains why slaveholders did not allow black slaves to worship and sing their songs unless authorised white people were present to proctor the meeting. And after the Nat Turner revolt, black preachers were declared illegal in most southern states. Black religious gatherings were often occasions for organising resistance against the institution of slavery.

Black history is the stuff out of which the black spirituals were created. But the 'stuff' of black history includes more than the bare historical facts of slavery. Black history is an experience, a soulful event. And to understand it is to know the Being of a people who had to 'feel their way along the course of American slavery,'[2] enduring the stresses and strains of human servitude but not without a song. *Black history is spiritual!*

Songs of Liberation

The divine liberation of the oppressed from slavery is the central theological concept in the black spirituals. These songs show that black slaves did not believe that human servitude was reconcilable with their African past and their knowledge of the Christian gospel. They did not believe that God created Africans to be the slaves of Europeans. Accordingly they sang of a God who was involved in history—*their* history—making right what whites have made wrong. Just as God delivered Moses and the Children of Israel from Egyptian bondage, drowning

Pharaoh and his army in the Red Sea, so also God will deliver black people from American slavery. It is this certainty that informs the thought of the black spirituals, enabling black slaves to sing:

Oh Mary, don't you weep, don't you moan,
Oh Mary, don't you weep, don't you moan.
Pharaoh's army got drownded,
Oh Mary, don't you weep.

The basic idea of the spirituals is that slavery contradicts God; it is a denial of the divine will. To be enslaved is to be declared a *nobody*, and that form of existence contradicts the creation of men and women to be God's children. Because black people believed that they were God's children, they affirmed their *somebodiness*, refusing to reconcile their servitude with divine revelation. They rejected white distortions of the gospel, which emphasised the obedience of slaves to their masters. They contended that God willed their freedom and not their slavery. That is why the spirituals focus on biblical passages that stress God's involvement in the liberation of oppressed people. Black people sang about Joshua and the battle of Jericho, Moses leading the Israelites from bondage, Daniel in the lion's den, and the Hebrew children in the fiery furnace. Here the emphasis is on God's liberation of the weak from the oppression of the strong, the lowly and downtrodden from the proud and mighty. And blacks reasoned that if God could lock the lion's jaw for Daniel and could cool the fire for the Hebrew children, then God could certainly deliver black people from slavery.

My Lord delivered Daniel
Why can't he deliver me?

Seeking to detract from the theological significance of the spirituals, some critics may point out that black slaves were literalists in their interpretation of the scripture, and this probably accounts for their acceptance of the white masters' interpretation of the Bible. Of course, it is true that slaves were not biblical critics and were unaware of erudite white reflections on the origins of biblical writings. Like most of their contemporaries, they accepted the inerrancy of Scripture. But the critical point is that their very literalism supported a black gospel of earthly freedom. They were literal when they sang about Daniel in the lions' den, David and Goliath, and Samson and the Philistines. On the other hand they dispensed with biblical literalism when white people began to use the curse of Ham and Paul as evidence that blacks ought to accept their slavery. As an ex-slave preacher put it:

'When I starts preaching I couldn't read or write and had to preach what Master told me, and he say tell them niggers iffen they obeys the master they goes to Heaven; but I knowed there's something better for them, but daren't tell them 'cept on the sly. That I done lots. I tells 'em iffen they keeps praying, the Lord will set 'em free.'[3]

It is significant that theology proper blends imperceptibly into the Christology of the spirituals. No theological distinction is made between the Son and the Father. Jesus is understood as the King, the deliverer of men and women from unjust suffering. He is the comforter in time of trouble, the lily of the valley and the bright and morning star.

He's King of Kings, He is Lord of Lords,
Jesus Christ the first and last,
No man works like him.

The death and resurrection of Jesus are particular focal points of the spirituals. The death of Jesus meant that the saviour died on the cross for black slaves. His death was a symbol of their suffering, their trials and tribulation in an unfriendly world. When Jesus was nailed to the cross and the Romans pierced him in the side, he was not alone; blacks suffered and died with him. That was why they sang.

Were you there when they crucified my Lord?
Were you there when they crucified my Lord?
Oh! Sometimes it causes me to tremble, tremble, tremble;
Were you there when they crucified my Lord?

Black slaves were there! Through the experience of being slaves, they encountered the theological significance of Jesus' death. With the crucifixion, Jesus makes an unqualified identification with the poor and helpless and takes their pain upon himself. They were there at the crucifixion because his death was for them.

And if Jesus was not alone in his suffering, they also were not alone in their slavery. Jesus is with them! Herein lies the meaning of the resurrection. It means that Jesus is not dead but is alive.

He rose, he rose, he rose from the dead, (3 times)
An' de Lord shall bear my spirit hom'.

The resurrection is the divine guarantee that their lives are in the hands of
him who conquered death, enabling the oppressed to do what is necessary
to remain obedient to God, the creator and sustainer of life.

Lament as affirmation

Though black slaves believed that the God of Jesus Christ was involved
in the historical liberation of oppressed people from bondgae, the continued
existence of American slavery seemed to contradict that belief. If God was
omnipotent and in control of human history, how could divine goodness
be reconciled with human servitude? If God had the power to deliver black
people from the evil of slavery as he delivered Moses from Pharaoh's army,
Daniel from the lion's den, and the Hebrew children from the fiery furnace,
why then were black slaves still subject to the rule of white masters? Why
are we still living in wretched conditions when God could end this evil
thing with one righteous stroke?

These are hard questions, and they are still relevant today. In the history
of theology and philosophy, these questions are the core of the 'problem of
evil', and college and seminary professors have spent many hours debating
them. But black slaves did not have the opportunity to investigate the
problem of suffering in the luxury of a seminary room with all the comforts
of modern living. They encountered suffering in the cotton fields of
Georgia, Arkansas, and Mississippi. Under the whip and pistol, they had
to deal with the absurdities of human existence. Every time they opened
their eyes and visualised the contradictions of their environment, they
realised they were 'rolling through an unfriendly world'. How could good
and powerful God be reconciled with white masters and overseers? What
explanation could the Holy One of Israel give for following the existence of
an ungodly slave institution?

In the spirituals the slaves' experience of suffering and despair defines
for them the major issue in their view of the world. The slaves do not
really question the justice and goodness of God, but rather take for granted
God's righteousness and vindication of the poor and weak. Indeed, it is the
point of departure for his or her faith. The slave has another concern,
centred on the faithfulness of the community of believers in a world full of
trouble. He or she wonders not whether God is just and right but whether
the sadness and pain of the world will cause the community to lose heart
and thus fall prey to the ways of evil. The slave is concerned about the

togetherness of the community of sufferers. Will the wretched of the earth be able to experience the harsh realities of despair and loneliness and take this pain upon themselves and not lose faith in the gospel of God? There was no attempt to evade the reality of suffering. Black slaves faced the reality of the world 'ladened wid trouble, an' burden'd wid grief', but they believed that they could go to Jesus in secret and get relief. They appealed to Jesus not so much to remove the trouble (though that was included), but to keep them from 'sinkin' down'.

Significantly, the note of despair is usually intertwined with confidence and joy that 'trouble don't last always'. To be sure, the slaves sang, 'Sometimes I feel like a motherless child, a long way from home'; but because they were confident that Jesus is with them and has not left them completely alone, they can still add (in the same song), 'True believer!' The black slaves did not deny the experience of agony and loneliness in a world filled with trouble.

Nobody knows de trouble I see,
Nobody knows but Jesus.
Nobody knows de trouble I see,
Glory, Hallelujah!

The 'Glory, Hallelujah!' is not a denial of trouble, it is an affirmation of faith. It says that despite the pain of being alone in an unfriendly world slaves were confident that God has not really left them, and *trouble* is not the last word on human existence.

Soon-a will be done with the troubles of the world;
Troubles of the world, troubles of the world,
Soon-a will be done with the troubles of the world;
Going home to live with God.

It appears that the slaves were not concerned with the problem of evil *per se*; they dealt with the world as it *is* not as it might have been if God had acted 'justly.' The slave focuses on present realities of despair and loneliness that disrupt the community of faith. When the faithful seem to have lost faith, one experiences the agony of being alone in a world of hardship and pain. That is why they sang.

An' I couldn't hear nobody pray, O Lord,
I couldn't hear nobody pray, O Lord,

O way down yonder by myself,
An' I couldn't hear nobody pray.

Related to the problem of suffering was the future, the 'not-yet' of black existence. How was it possible for black slaves to take seriously their pain and suffering in an unfriendly world and still believe that God was liberating them from earthly bondage? How could they *really* believe that God was just when they knew only injustice and oppression? The answer to these questions lies in the concept of heaven, which is the dominant idea in black religious experience as expressed in the black spirituals.

Heaven and human dignity

The concept of heaven in black religion has not been interpreted rightly. Most observers have defined the black religious experience exclusively in terms of slaves longing for heaven as if that desire was unrelated to their earthly liberation. It has been said that the concept of heaven served as an opiate for black slaves, making for docility and submission. But to interpret black eschatology solely in terms of its outmoded cosmology fails to take seriously the culture and thought of a people seeking expression amidst the dehumanisation of slavery. It is like discarding the Bible and its message as irrelevant because the biblical writers had a three-stoned conception of the universe. While not all biblical and systematic theologians agree with Rudolf Bultmann's method of demythologisation in his efforts to solve the problem of biblical mythology, most agree that he is correct in his insistence that the gospel message is not dependent on its pre-scientific world-picture. Is it not possible that the same analogy is true in regard to the heaven theme in the spirituals?

The place to begin is Miles Fisher's contention that the spirituals are primarily 'historical documents'. They tell us about the black movement for historical liberation, the attempt of black people to define their present history in the light of their promised future, not according to their past miseries. Fisher notes that heaven for early black slaves referred not only to a transcendent reality beyond time and space; it designated the earthly places that blacks regarded as lands of freedom. Heaven referred to Africa, Canada, and the states north of the Mason-Dixon line.[4] Frederick Douglass wrote about the double meaning of these songs:

'We were at times remarkably buoyant, singing hymns, and making

joyous exclamations, almost as triumphant in their tone as if we had
reached a land of freedom and safety. A keen observer might have
detected in our repeated singing of

O Canaan, sweet Canaan,
I am bound for the land of Canaan,

something more than a hope of reaching heaven. We meant to reach the
North, and the North was our Canaan.[5]

But while it is true that heaven had its historical referents, not all black
slaves could hope to make it to Africa, Canada, or even to the northern
section of the United States. Black slaves began to realise that their
historical freedom could not be assured as long as white racists controlled
the governmental process of America. And so, they found it necessary to
develop a style of freedom that included but did not depend upon
historical possibilities. What could freedom mean for black slaves who
could never expect to participate in the determination of society's laws
governing their lives? Must they continue to define freedom in terms of
the possibility of escape and insurrection as if their humanity depended
on their willingness to commit suicide? It was in response to this situation
that the black concept of heaven developed.

For black slaves, who were condemned to carve out their existence in
human captivity, heaven meant that the eternal God has made decision
about their humanity that could not be destroyed by white slavemasters.
Whites could drive them, beat them, even kill them; but they believed that
God nevertheless had chosen black slaves as God's own and that this
election bestowed upon them a freedom to *be*, which could not be measured
by what oppressors could do to the physical body.

The idea of heaven provided ways for black people to affirm their
humanity when other people were attempting to define them as non-
persons. It enabled blacks to say 'yes' to their right to be free by affirming
God's eschatological freedom to be for the oppressed. That was what they
meant when they sang about a 'city called heaven.'

I am a poor pilgrim of sorrow.
I'm tossed in this wide world alone.
No hope have I for tomorrow.
I'm trying to make heaven my home.

Sometimes I am tossed and driven, Lord.
Sometimes I don't know where to roam.
I've heard of a city called heaven.
I started to make it my home.

In the midst of economic and political disfranchisement, black slaves held themselves together and did not lose their spiritual composure because they believed that their worth transcended governmental decisions. That was why they looked forward to 'walking to Jerusalem just like John' and longed for the 'camp meeting in the promised land'.

Despite the ways which black eschatology might have been misused or the crude forms in which it was sometimes expressed, it was primarily a theological perspective on the present which enabled oppressed blacks to realise that their existence transcended historical limitations. This emphasis is, perhaps, the most important contribution of black religion as reflected in the spirituals. Far from being poignant expressions of shattered humanity, they were affirmations of hope—hope that enabled black slaves to risk their lives for earthly freedom because they knew they had a home 'over yonder'.

Notes

1. *The Gift of Black Folk* (New York 1970), p. 158. Originally published in 1924.
2. Comment by Guy Johnson of the University of North Carolina, cited in Sterling Stuckey, 'Through the Prism of Folklore', in *Black and White in American Culture*, ed. J. Chametyky and S. Kaplan (Amherst 1969), p. 172.
3. B. A. Botkin, ed., *Lay My Burden Down* (Chicago 1945), p. 26.
4. Fisher, *Negro Slave Songs in the United States* (New York 1953), Chaps. 1–4.
5. *Life and Times of Frederick Douglass* (New York 1962), p. 159. A reprint of the 1892 revised edition.

Editor's Note

The versions of spirituals presented in this discussion may be found in one of the following sources: James Weldon Johnson and J. Rosamond Johnson, *The Book of American Negro Spirituals* (New York 1925; 1969 ed.); John Work, ed., *American Negro Songs and Spirituals* (New York 1940); *Religious Folk Songs of the Negro* (Hampton; Va. 1920); Edward Boatner, compiler, *Thirty Afro-American Choral Spirituals* (1964). 'O Mary, Don't you Weep' is recorded by the Utica Jubilee Singers on *From Jubilee to Gospel: A Selection of Commercially Recorded Black Religious Music,*

1921–1953, selected and annotated by William Tallmadge (JEMF-108, 1980); 'He Rose From the Dead' is recorded on *The Fisk Jubilee Singers: Negro Spirituals* (Folkways: FA2372, 1955).

Mellonee Burnim

The Performance of Black Gospel Music as Transformation

ANYONE WHO has regularly attended gospel music performance events can attest to the existence of seemingly formulaic combinations of actions, words and musical motifs in performance. Choirs dress in bold vibrant colours, soloists give spoken testimonies of their unique experiences of God, and congregations provide verbal feedback at the precise moment when something of particular significance occurs in the performance.

Perhaps some would misinterpret these ritual acts as an indicator of musical stagnation or spiritual lack within the black community. As a result, they may opt to either turn off or tune out the experience of gospel music altogether. Even so, the numbers of those joining the ranks of gospel supporters and performers grow daily. Gospel music has moved beyond the worship of the Pentecostals and Baptists to become a central component of the liturgies of Black Methodist, Catholic and Episcopalian churches. Gospel music is no longer simply 5 a.m. radio listening for the early morning riser; now it can be heard on 24-hour gospel radio stations, on national TV, in movie theatres and at symphony orchestra concerts as well.

But how much do we really understand about gospel music's meaning and significance as an indigenous form of black musical expression? The body of scholarly inquiry into this musical genre has hardly scratched the surface. The complexities of gospel music are many, and they beg the attention of serious scholars who are willing to dig deeply in the search for its cultural and spiritual meaning.

Two approaches to study

In an effort to develop an accurate and culturally relevant characterisation of the gospel music tradition, the ensuing discussion utilises the emic approach, succinctly defined by the ethnicity scholar George De Vos as

'an attempt on the part of the scientific observer to understand the conceptual system of the observed and to state his observations as best he can within the conceptual framework of the observed.'[1]

The early history of ethnomusicology was plagued, however, with interpretations of musical culture generated by an 'etic' approach which 'analyses an observed situation in terms of the external system of the observer'.[2] Black music has been an acute and prolonged victim of the etic approach, sometimes even at the hands of those who are members of the culture. This tragedy occurs when the cultural insider, wilfully or not, imposes an alien perspective on black music traditions.

This discussion views gospel as a unique form of musical expression, created *by* black people, *for* black people, and subject to valid criticism and analysis only from the vantage point of a black cultural framework. Black Americans perceive gospel music as a profoundly black tradition which contributes significantly to the distinction between black and white religious practices in the United States. Accordingly, gospel music clearly functions as a symbol of ethnicity for Black Americans.[3]

I have written elsewhere on the conceptual unity which governs the performance of gospel music, illustrating how an ideological and an aesthetic framework defines every aspect of performance—from the physical mode of presentation to the timbre of the voice or instrument, to the actual musical mechanics.[4] This unified conceptual framework also embraces the idea of change, of transformation—the process of becoming something different from what was before. Through attitudinal adjustments, often triggered by verbal cues, physical structures can be spiritually transformed. Through a union of various cultural signs and symbols, individuals can be led to an experience of altered states of being. The present analysis will explore the processes of change or transformation which characterise the gospel music tradition. The study seeks to codify patterns of behavior which point to the existence of an underlying system of cultural values among Black Americans in the United States. The two processes of change which I will explore are: (1) Transformation of Personae; and (2) Transformation of Space.

The transformation of personae

In understanding the depth and complexity of black gospel music performance and all of its ramifications, I have analysed this musical complex from the standpoint of history, ritual and interaction, those three sources which Orrin Klapp[5] designates as primary contributors to the development of a collective ethnic identity. All three components are integrally linked, mutually influencing one another in the process of a people carving out and establishing its identity. Klapp's thesis, as summarised by Dashefsky and Shapiro, is as follows:

> *History* shows conflicts that increase distinctions between in-groups and out-groups and symbols (names, places, heroes) that bestow collective identity of members of the group. *Ritual* and ceremony feed back to the people as a whole the facts and fiction of their historical experience. *Social interaction* provides a continual daily flow under the uneven tide of history and ritual, reminding people of their shared experience and their common perspectives on life.[6]

The key element in exploring transformational processes in gospel music is to view the performance event as ritual. Because gospel music was spawned and nurtured in the context of ritual, performers are virtually impelled, in all performance settings, to recreate the climate of the black worship service.

The performer of black religious music holds an incumbent responsibility to communicate on two levels—culturally and spiritually—and to share this communication with two separate receiving units—God and the listening congregation. One critical dimension of performance in gospel music is what I have termed in my research on the black gospel music aesthetic as 'style of delivery'.[7] In other words, the physical manner in which the song is presented carries symbolic relevance for the congregation as it evaluates the quality of a given performance.

The style of delivery in the black musical aesthetic includes the following aspects of performance: dress, facial expression, gestures, religious dance, and performer-audience interplay. If one chooses to analyse gospel music performance from a purely spiritual point of view, these variables may well be considered extraneous appendages. However, in seeking to understand the cultural dimensions of gospel music performance, it is again instructive to refer to analytical models of social science which treat the concept of ethnic identity.

Frederick Barth, for example, outlines two categories through which ethnic groups can be distinguished: (1) overt signs and symbols, and (2) basic value orientations. The first category includes 'the diacritical features that people look for and exhibit to show identity' such as dress, language, house form or general style of life. The second category encompasses standards of morality and excellence by which performance is judged.[8]

In the realm of gospel music performance the element of dress functions in two ways: (1) as a means of distinguishing one in-group from another— a device for establishing small group identity (choir/ensemble) within the larger group (black); and (2) as a symbol of the cultural value of dressing well, 'looking good', or 'styling' and profiling'. The latter concept applies to both performer and congregation, who put on their 'Sunday-go-to-meetin' best' for a gospel concert, even if it's not held on Sunday, and even if it is not staged in a church.[9] When the distinctive costume, or outfit, fits neatly into the black 'universe of meaning,' the clothes themselves can play an important role in transforming or translating both performer and audience into a world which contrasts with the ordinary, and affirms cultural identity. It has been determined that 'identifiable thoughts, images and associations begin to crystallise around clothing symbols', although the meaning may vary markedly among subsets of the larger group.[10]

To have a complete personal, transforming experience of God, performers must certainly do more than dress well. This visual dimension of gospel music is only one factor in the total complex. Another aspect of physical transformation in gospel music performance exists in the realm of kinetics, or body movement. Mahalia Jackson has repeatedly expressed how she used her hands and feet—her whole body—when she sang.[11] Mahalia is representative of a broad spectrum of gospel singers whose performance style is overtly demonstrative. In contrast, there is an equally strong contingent of gospel singers who choose to sing 'flat footed', oftentimes with eyes closed. The closing of the eyes is not intended to shut off communication with the congregation, but is directed toward opening up communion with God. As one respondent commented in viewing a gospel performance video-recorded during my fieldwork,

> Now these people [the Bishop's Choir], when they come upstairs [fol-lowing prayer] they don't care about the audience. . . . This is to Him and they're not going to half step! The main goal is to draw people to Christ through their songs. If nobody hears them, but *God* hears them, I believe that they don't care!'[12]

The important ingredient to the seasoned black listener is the performer's communication of sincerity, that the presentation be 'convincing'.[13]

Members of the congregation look for evidence that the performer is 'gettin' into' the song, a syntactic phrase which implies a *process of becoming*, or the transformation of the individual or group from one state of being to another.

Within this broad framework, performers have considerable latitude in expressing themselves. The equation is complete when the congregation responds with verbal and physical affirmation during the performance. While one may shout 'Praise the Lord', still another may simply wave a hand or shed a tear. The congregation has not merely been engaged, but inspired; they too have become participants in the transformational process.

These overt behavioral symbols of the transformation of the individual are mere low-level, or at best, intermediary steps directed toward the ultimate experience of spiritual transformation. Spiritual preparation for the performance begins with prayer, be it verbalised or silent, be it inside the physical structure or elsewhere. The performer who 'comes for service' spends time in personal communion with God before a note is ever struck or sung. Prayer in the gospel music domain therefore functions minimally in two ways: (1) to prepare or sanctify the physical environment and (2) to prepare the individual performer for deep and intense spiritual communion with God.

During the 1930s, the National Convention of Gospel Choirs and Choruses was co-founded by Thomas A. Dorsey, Sallie Martin, and Mother Willie Mae Ford Smith for the purpose of performing and disseminating gospel music. The film *Say Amen, Somebody* documents the contributions and perspectives of these pioneers. In it, Mother Smith contends that the *ultimate* goal of the gospel performer is 'anointed singing'. Functioning as head of the solo division of the convention, she cautions her audience during a working session: 'that's what the world don't understand about gospel singing; it's a *different* singing when you're *anointed* to sing'.

Just as the sequence of events in a gospel music performance spirals systematically from low to high gear, the variables of dress, kinetics and prayer are all contributors to the peak religious experience of what black people refer to as 'shouting' or 'getting happy'. This altered state of consciousness, which represents the ultimate spiritual transformation, is often so valued among some gospel practitioners that they consciously seek to manipulate those variables which contribute to achieving this state. As I was told during my field research: 'like [some] churches and stuff, I think they *mean* to be singing for God, but they be singing for the people'.[14]

Such contrived efforts do not diminish the depth of meaning which total immersion in gospel music performance—culturally and spiritually—can bring to both performer and audience. Within this realm of spiritual transformation lies the greatest potential for truly inspired performances; where sopranos and tenors reach notes in their ranges that they've never before reached, where textual interjections and interpolations become most imaginative and poignant, and where musical phrasings assume a creative twist which may never be repeated again in quite the same way.

Mother Willie Mae Ford Smith sheds further light on this heightened dimension of gospel performance, in her discussion in *Say Amen, Somebody* of how text plays such an important role in the gospel equation.

'Enunciation is the main thing. Gospel singing must be thoroughly understood. If you're going to sing the gospel, you must let it be a *spell* you cast on the people with your enunciation' [emphasis mine].

The transformation is complete when the spiritual 'message' has been received. A process which begins as a personal communion with God through song becomes communal as the congregation is drawn into the experience. The cultural symbols of dress and expressive behavior are mere catalysts to achieving total 'surrender' in the experience of God.

Transformation of space

In the minds of avid gospel supporters, black gospel music is as much about the *experience* of the music as about the performance of it. Whether performances are held in prisons, on college campuses or in massive municipal auditoriums, gospel music is viewed by black Christians as an aspect of worship. John Mbiti describes a similar concept in his analysis of African religions:

We may conclude that there is no limit as to where and when African peoples perform one or more acts of worship. God is omnipresent, and he is 'reachable' at any time and any place. People worship Him where and whenever the 'need' arises. Set times and places are only the result of regular usage: they are not rules regulating worship as such, and do not impose any limit to man's contact with God and the spiritual world.'[15]

The concept of the personal, omnipresent God was clearly evident in the worship of African slaves in the New World. Attempts of slave masters to prevent religious activity among them were circumvented by holding meetings in secluded places—woods, gullies, ravines and thickets—the 'invisible church'.[16]

It is precisely this ability to transform space which has been transferred to contemporary performances of Black gospel music. Before beginning the concert 'proper' at the annual anniversary songfest of the Bishop's Choir (a 75-member group of men and women between the ages of 16 and 35, who are members of Grace Apostolic Church, Indianapolis, Indiana), there was a devotional service—a period of prayer, meditation and personal testimony—which established the consecrated milieu. Similarly, performances in contexts other than churches are prefaced with prayer. The place where the prayer is offered is not important—parking lot, dressing room, or backstage—nor is the actual length of the prayer of great essence. The inclusion of the prayer as an essential, not optional component, at both performances and rehearsals, is a strong indicator of the view of performance as worship, no matter what the context.

Not all efforts to transform secular contexts to sacred ones are readily identifiable, especially to the cultural outsider. Less apparent are those metaphysical processes which often occur as mere verbal cues indicating the valued attitude or approach to the musical/spiritual event. For example, the admonition 'We didn't come to put on a show; we came to have church!' has become so widespread at gospel music performance events that the avid gospel supporter comes both to expect and to accept this frame of reference. Only those for whom a secular setting signifies a secular event—those who are unaware of the ritual aspects of gospel music—are surprised or annoyed by the omnipresent religious overtones of all gospel music performances.

Such was the case when I overheard the following comment of a non-black audience member at the 1979 spring concert of a local gospel choir, the Indiana University Voices of Hope: 'I really like the music, but I just wish they would cut out all that Jesus stuff'. For this uninitiated observer, the mini-sermonettes interspersed between songs during the concert, which established the spiritual continuity of the programme, were a mere distraction, not an ingredient essential for the formulation of a conceptual whole.

The Gospel Music Worship of America, founded by its current president, the Reverend James Cleveland, was created in 1969, becoming a contemporary counterpart of the National Convention of Gospel Choirs and Choruses mentioned above. Tens of thousands of participants from across the united States attend this convention annually. Despite the prevailing festival spirit which seems to dominate the atmosphere at this week-long gospel extravaganza, there is a strong, well-defined spiritual undercurrent which shapes every aspect of the scheduled activities. Cleveland demands an air of reverence and respects during *All* 'services'; anyone who fails to comply faces public chastisement and humiliation. In fact, the extensive use of the word 'service' to designate events devoted expressly to music, represents a conscious rejection of such terms as 'concert' or 'performance' by black participants. Whereas the label 'service' properly identifies the ritual context, the latter designations hold non-sacred connotations considered misleading and therefore undesirable by many worshippers. That is to say, one goes to a 'concert' to be entertained; one goes to a 'service' to praise God.

During a performance at the Indianapolis Convention Center in the summer of 1978, well-known gospel soprano Sarah Jordan Powell suddenly interrupted her testimony to address a request to technicians that the house lights be turned on. Having felt too distant—too far removed from her audience— Powell explained 'I like to *see* who I'm talking to'.[17] Sarah Jordan Powell was acutely aware that worship in the context of the typical black church structure minimised the distance between performer and congregation, thereby facilitating the expressive dialogue between the two which characterises Black worship. When the congregation responds with verbal affirmations of 'Amen', 'Sing, chile', and 'That's all right', during the performance, the singer is encouraged to greater, often spectacular, musical heights. In order for Ms Powell to recreate or approximate this religious milieu, it was necessary for the physical space to be transformed to permit visual contact between performer and audience, just as there would be in a church.

An example of how space is physically transformed to establish symbolically the desired spiritual climate occurs annually at the National Convention of Gospel Choirs and Choruses. In the film *Say Amen, Somebody*, which documents the opening consecration service, the space is prepared for worship by draping the furniture (chairs, pulpit and altar) in the massive auditorium in white. The ritual symbolises the cleansing process required to transform the site into a house of worship. By executing this service at the beginning of the convention, the spiritual milieu which is to govern the entire week is clearly established from the outset.

Because gospel music is so frequently performed outside the confines of the church building, black people consciously engage in ritual acts and dialogue to express their religious intent. Efforts to transform secular contexts to sacred ones can occur at both the physical and metaphysical level. For black supporters of gospel music, space is not self-defining; quite the opposite, *content* is the key to defining *context*.

Conclusion

Because the gospel music is a tradition created by and for Black Americans, it is a unique expression of black values, black experiences, and black beliefs. Those in attendance at gospel music events are thereby governed, whether they can realise it or not, by the dictates of black religious ritual. Even if concert goers have been attracted to the event primarily by the gospel music *sound* rather than by religious devotion (as many admittedly are), participants must nonetheless conform to the rules of behaviour sanctioned by the black church.

This ritual dimension of performance is the major factor which distinguishes gospel music from secular music traditions within black culture. Although the same aesthetic principles apply to performance of both sacred and secular musics,[18] performances of gospel music are governed by an underlying religious or spiritual *intent*. When this religious dimension of gospel music is lost or negated, the real meaning and significance of this music genre is lost as well.

In-depth study of gospel music performance reveals a complex exchange or dialogue between performer, congregation and God. The conceptual framework which directs this dialogue is crouched in layers of symbolism often not understood or even apparent to the outsider. It is clear from the research that seasoned participants in the gospel music tradition fully understand the significance of these transactions. Accordingly, transformations of space and personae are perceived as processes essential for completion of the spiritual communication network. Transformational processes in black gospel music performance are a dynamic indicator of the richness and vitality of a culture constantly engaging in systematic processes of regeneration and creativity.

Notes

1. George De Vos, 'Ethnic Pluralism: Conflict and Accommodation', in his *Ethnic Identity: Cultural Continuities and Change* (California 1975), p. 17.

2. *Ibid.*, p. 17.

3. The concept of gospel music as a cultural symbol is developed fully in my dissertation entitled 'The Black Gospel Musical Tradition: Symbol of Ethnicity', PhD dissertation, Indiana University, 1980.

4. Mellonee Burnim, 'The Black Gospel Music Tradition: A Complex of Ideology, Aesthetic and Behavior', in *More Than Dancing*, ed. Irene Jackson (Westport, Conn. 1985).

5. Orrin Klapp, *Currents of Unrest: An Introduction to Collective Behavior* (New York 1962).

6. Arnold Dashefsky and Howard M. Shapiro, 'Collective Search for Ethnic Identity', in *Ethnic Identity and Society*, ed. Arnold Dashefsky (Chicago 1976), pp. 197–200.

7. For a detailed discussion of the Black gospel music aesthetic, see Burnim, *op. cit.*

8. Frederick Barth, *Ethnic Groups and Boundaries* (Boston 1969), p. 14.

9. Mellonee Burnim, 'Functional Dimensions of Gospel Music Performance', *Western Journal of Black Studies* (in press).

10. Fred Davis, 'Clothing and Fashion as Communication', in *The Psychology of Fashion*, ed. Michael Solomon (Lexington, Mass. 1985), pp. 18–19.

11. Mahalia Jackson, *Movin' On Up* (New York 1966), pp. 65–66.

12. Keith Scott, *et al.,* Feedback Interview, 17 October 1979, Indiana University, Bloomington. Methodology consisted of respondents providing spontaneous commentary on gospel music event which I video-recorded during fieldwork in 1979–80.

13. *Ibid.*

14. *Ibid.*

15. John Mbiti, *African Religions and Philosophy*, 1969, Garden City (New York 1970), pp. 95–96.

16. Albert Raboteau, *Slave Religion*, 1978 (New York 1980), p. 215.

17. Sarah Jordan Powell, Concert of Gospel Music with Carl Preacher, Walter Hawkins and the Family, and Andrae Crouch, Convention Center, Indianapolis, Indiana, July 1978.

18. See Mellonee Burnim and Portia Maultsby 'From Backwoods to City Streets: The Afro-American Musical Journey', in *Expressively Black*, eds. Geneva Gay and Willie Baber (New York 1987), pp. 109–135.

David Dargie

Xhosa Church Music

The Xhosa

THE XHOSA are the so-called 'Bantu' Nguni people who inhabit the southernmost part of Africa, the Cape Province of South Africa, as far as the Natal border. They include some twelve chiefdom clusters, all of whom use the Xhosa language and belong to the Xhosa cultural area. All have much in common in their music and rituals.

The Xhosa language is characterised by its click consonants, one of which ('x') occurs in their name. These clicks, and other elements of Xhosa language and culture, were absorbed from the KhoiSan ('Hottentot' and 'Bushman') peoples who in former times also populated the area. The Xhosas (whose name in Khoi means 'angry people') have a long history of resistance to white intrusion, from the first important clashes in 1702 to the last Frontier War of 1878. It was largely from the Xhosas that the African National Congress was born in 1912. The A.N.C. was founded not to fight the whites but to have a dialogue with them, in order to try to obtain civil rights for the black population. It was only when the Sharpeville massacre of 1960 convinced many blacks that dialogue was useless that the A.N.C. turned to violent methods. Prominent Xhosa people include Nelson Mandela, the late Steve Biko, and the Nobel Peace Prize winner Archbishop Desmond Tutu of the Anglican Church.

Music in Xhosa life

Ironically music is so important in Xhosa community life that there is no Xhosa word for music. Like most African peoples, the Xhosa do not abstract ideas such as music. All their musical terminology reflects the human and community aspects of music. There is no word for music, but there are words for songs and for the community events which involve song. There is no word meaning simply 'to sing'. There are words which mean to lead the song, to follow the song, to sing with clapping, to sing with clapping for others (to dance), to dance with participation in the song. In traditional Xhosa there is no word for 'composer'. The present-day dictionary word in fact means someone who composes song texts.

Traditionally the Xhosas know the Great God, called uQamata, uThixo and other names. He is usually not approached directly, except in times of drought and national crisis, when prayers to uQamata were (and still are) led on the mountain by the chief. Normally traditional religion uses the ancestral shades either as intermediaries with uQamata or themselves as protectors and helpers of the living. All rites and ceremonies of traditional religion have their own particular songs and dance styles. There are rites for all important occasions of individual and community life—initiation, marriage, and the various ceremonies (including divination) which put people in touch with the ancestors. There are also ritual dance-gatherings for all the different peer groups: diviners, men and women, women only, young men and young women, boys and girls. All the members of each peer-group are involved in the respective ritual songs, which play a vital role in the building up of the community as a whole, and the communities within the larger community. In addition, certain ritual gatherings involve the whole community—village or region.

The First Xhosa Christian

The first Christian missionary to preach to the Xhosa was the Congregational, Dr J. Van der Kemp, in 1799. He made no converts. However, some fifteen years later, in the context of heightening conflict between Xhosas and white settlers, Ntsikana son of Gabha, one of chief Ngqika's councillors, remembering Van der Kemp's teaching, underwent conversion. While he was dancing at a wedding a great wind blew, stopping the dance. Ntsikana went home with his family, and sat up all night singing a new song. In the morning he had a vision of strange light, and told people something had entered him which said all must pray to the Great God. He began to preach, expressing the Christian truths in African terms.

He gathered a group of disciples, who were allowed, contrary to common missionary practice, to live in their own village. He interpreted the events of his time with Christian insight, warning against a certain attack on the settlers, and against internecine strife among the Xhosa. The warnings were ignored, with disastrous results for Xhosa power, so that today his followers still call him Ntsikana the prophet.

Of particular interest here is that Ntsikana composed Christian songs for the worship services he conducted daily for his disciples. On his death-bed in 1821 he sent his followers to join the new London Missionary Society (Presbyterian) mission at Tyhume near the present town of Alice. With them the disciples took his story, his preaching, and his songs. His Great Hymn was written down for the first time in 1822. It has since been featured in all the main Xhosa hymn books (except the Catholic).

This remarkable hymn, still used today in the churches, expresses Christian truths in the style of an African praise poem. God is the True Shield. He is the Great Blanket which we put on. He hunts for souls, he reconciles flocks which fight with each other. His hands and feet are wounded, his blood poured out for us. Are we worthy of such a great price? The hymn also uses Xhosa musical style. It retains scale and harmony based on the Xhosa musical bows. Even more remarkable, the hymn has survived as a traditional song, sung in various ways, with Xhosa rhythm, call-and-response forms, and with musical accompaniment. Interestingly, it has found its way also into traditional religion.

Largely thanks to Ntsikana, Christian influence has been strong among the Xhosa. Many belong to main-line churches (there are possibly 300,000 Catholics today out of 5 to 6 million Xhosa people). Perhaps even more belong to locally-founded indigenous churches. And many who belong to no formal denomination call themselves 'AmaGqobokha'—the converts— and owe allegiance to Christ in some way. Ntsikana's hymn therefore has a special significance for the Xhosa people. It is a national song, with nationalist implications. In 1909 a general meeting of the Xhosa chose Ntsikana as a national hero, ahead of great chiefs such as Hintsa, Sarhili and Sandile. It was from the ranks of the St Ntsikana Memorial Association that many founding members of the A.N.C. came.

In one version of the hymn there is internal evidence that it was a patriotic song during the War of Mlanjeni in 1850. The writings of Ntsikana's disciples and their successors (such as the Rev Tiyo Soga) mention the great emotional effect the hymn had on Xhosa congregations during the times of the Frontier Wars. Two forms of the hymn (the 'Bell' and the Great Hymn) were sung at the installation of Desmond Tutu as Anglican Archbishop of Cape Town.

Mission music and its problems

The missionaries deserve great admiration for their pioneering work. They were often caught between the colonial government (which resented their efforts to uplift the oppressed) and the Xhosa nationalists (who saw them as colonial agents). At least one Anglican mission was burnt by British troops during the war of 1878.

Regrettably, however, the missionaries saw little of value in African culture. Despite Ntsikana's example, it seems they never considered inviting their converts to compose their own hymns in Xhosa style. In church use, Ntsikana's hymn was divested of African rhythm and form, retaining only its original melody and harmony. To provide additional church music the missionaries turned first to Xhosa translations of European hymns, later also using non-metrical chants. In time many Xhosas were taught to compose (in sol-fa) in the largely diatonic and rhythmless Victorian choir style. All these musical manifestations are still very much part of Xhosa Christianity. Sometimes the results of even this Victorian composition were excellent, for example the great *Nkosi sikelel' iAfrika* (Lord bless Africa) by Enoch Sontonga, which will very likely be the National Anthem of a liberated South Africa.

The first Catholic missions to the Xhosa came much later. In 1880 the Trappists founded Dunbrody mission near Port Elizabeth. When they moved on to Mariannhill in the Zulu area, the Jesuits took over (1882), and also founded Keilands mission on the Kei River (1884). Dunbrody did not endure, but Keilands is still going strong. The main Catholic drive came only in the 1920's and later, the early Catholic ventures being aimed chiefly at a settler church.

For many years Catholic missionaries were content to follow Protestant musical examples, with Catholic variations. Now Xhosas could sing the Lourdes hymn and 'O Bread of Heaven' in Xhosa, and the *Tantum Ergo* in Latin to the tune of 'My Darling Clementine'.

Because African languages are tonal, singing African texts to the wrong music either alters the meaning of the words or renders them meaningless. Because of this the hymns have been described by one critic as 'completely meaningless. All of them. They are quite incomprehensible to an outsider'.[1] Regrettably, most African Christians have not questioned what has been imposed for so long in their churches, because missionaries 'have assiduously taught Africans to sing the sacred gibberish for so long that even the most educated of them have accepted this nonsensical convention'.[2]

What was done to rhythm was even more destructive. The missionaries realised that the accent patterns did not fit the Xhosa language, but rather than turn to Xhosa rhythm they developed the rhythmless psalm-tones. With their misunderstanding and horror of African dancing, they determined by all means to keep all body movement, clapping or other rhythmic manifestations out of church music. Missionaries even took the liberty of altering the language in order to impose European music theory. A word which formerly meant to 'sing little songs' was turned to mean 'to sing while keeping still'. This was the stem -*cula*, so that today in church and school *ukucula* means 'to sing', *iculo* is a hymn, and *umculo* means 'music'.

Not only was the idea of music now abstracted, but the introduction of the use of church choirs effectively took participation in worship music away from most members of the ordinary congregations. The Western hymns were too strange for ordinary people to join in—they had to be performed by specialists—a far cry from traditional ritual. Choir competitions were introduced, and are still bedevilling African churches, with discord and jealousy entering in in ways not found in traditional music. Two recent such competitions have actually led to rioting.

White domination in church, and African rebellion

It is an ongoing problem that the priest, and even more the missionary, tends to dominate his congregation. In order to create church leadership roles for themselves, certain black Christians in the nineteenth century founded independent churches. Some of these took as their model the Coptic Church of Ethiopia, usually retaining main-line church worship and music, but establishing black control. The best-known of these is the Order of Ethiopia, which re-affiliated with the Anglicans.

Other independent foundations took as their ideal Biblical Zion, with great emphasis on the role of the Holy Spirit. Perhaps over two million of these Zionists congregate at Moria in the Northern Transvaal every Easter. Many Xhosas belong to a variety of Zionist congregations. The Zionists are noted for their indigenous liturgies, which use African songs with drums and rhythmic instruments, body movement and clapping. In recent times, as African control of main-line churches has grown, many congregations of Methodists have begun to develop their own songs, using clapping and rhythmic beating of hymn-books and cushions. Other denominations have followed their example, and a large number of songs are now shared between Anglicans, Protestants and Zionists, using African rhythm to a greater or lesser extent. This music has begun reaching Catholics too, though it has taken a quarter of a century to penetrate from the meeting room into church.

The Catholic bishops' pastoral plan, and Lumko Institute: music as a community builder

Lumko Missiological Institute was launched as a language training institute for missionaries in 1962. It absorbed the catechist school already existing at Lumko mission, 60 kilometres east of Queenstown in the Xhosa Thembu area and in time it developed as a centre for training lay church leaders, offering materials and courses in ministries training. With the example of Latin America and other parts of Africa, Lumko began to focus on the task of building up the Church as a community of small or basic Christian communities. Perhaps the main figure in shaping the direction of Lumko, and producing much of its published materials, was Fr Fritz Lobinger, a secular priest of the German diocese of Regensburg, who is now the bishop of Aliwal North (also in the Xhosa region). Lobinger has been one of the leading theologians assisting the Southern African Catholic Bishops Conference in formulating the Pastoral Plan which is presently being brought into action in the Church in South Africa. This Pastoral Plan views the Church as a community of communities serving humanity. Its focus is on making active the local church communities under local leadership, making the laity effective in bringing the Church to life. This is also Lumko's vision of the Church, for which Lumko has various departments focusing on pastoral and ministries training, group Gospel sharing as a community-building exercise, and on social awareness in the South African context. Lumko's vision is of 'a model of the Church as a community of small Christian communities which are truly local, Bible-based, socially aware and active' (Fr R. F. Broderick, rector of Lumko in 1988). (In 1985 Lumko Institute moved to Germiston, Transvaal.)

In 1964, Fritz Lobinger and Oswald Hirmer (who is now one of the priests on the staff of Lumko), then working as missionaries in the diocese of Aliwal North, commissioned the best-known Xhosa composer of his day, the sol-fist B. K. Tyamzashe, to compose music in Xhosa style for the Catholic Church. For inspiration, Tyamzashe, who had never had such a request before, turned to Ntsikana. Among the many successful church songs he produced was the famous *Gloria* of his *Missa I*, published in 1965. In 1966, working in the parish of Zwelitsha, I encouraged the choir and its leader Mr L. Mpotulo to use the new *Missa I*, with striking results. Largely due to the impact of Xhosa music in church, when I left Zwelitsha in 1967 the congregation had doubled.

In 1977, to obtain new songs for the new Xhosa hymn book (of which Hirmer was editor), I held a composition workshop in Zwelitsha (having seen the method in Zimbabwe). The church singers present produced some

53 compositions in a week-end, many of which are still being sung. The success of this and other similar workshops led Lumko to open a church music department in 1979. In addition to the several hundred new songs in Xhosa produced since then, this work has spread throughout the Catholic Church in South Africa. To date Lumko has published over a hundred tapes of new African church music in 20 languages.

An important venture was the introduction of marimba xylophones as church music instruments. Hirmer imported the first from Zimbabwe at the request of Lambert Mpotulo, choir master of Zwelitsha. These were adapted to Xhosa scale, and are now built in Umtata in the Xhosa area. Over a hundred sets of marimbas are now in use in parishes in Southern Africa.

It is no doubt excellent that now many congregations are using attractive genuinely African songs, incorporating African rhythm and other musical concepts. What is of greater value to the Church is that through music local congregations are able to contribute to their own development as basic Christian communities. Not only is the music accessible to all who attend worship, it is also something given by themselves for the glory of God. It may take time for many congregations to accept the change: the fallacy of the superiority of European ways takes time to erode. But Black Consciousness and related movements in South Africa are engendering in the local people a growth of self-respect, which the Church is trying by all means to foster. It is significant that in recent times more and more liberation prayers are incorporated in the new church music compositons.

The new songs, and the use of marimbas, have successfully involved African youth in their Church. Similar results were shown by work in Munich in 1988, when African church songs were learned with great enthusiasm (in German) by young Catholics. Church songs will certainly be part of Africa's contribution to the re-vitalisation of the Church.

Conclusion

The example of Ntsikana shows that Western education is not a necessary pre-requisite for successfully conducting mission work. Africans can successfully plant the gospel in their own regions, and through the genius of their culture can also contribute to the universal mission effort.

Just as the Christian churches stand by the Xhosa and other peoples of South Africa in their struggle for civil and political rights, so too should the Church play a part in the cultural liberation of the people. The results can only benefit the World Church.

References

Xhosa history, language and religion
J. B. Peires, *The House of Phalo* (Johannesburg 1981).
John Milton, *The Edges of War* (Cape Town 1983).
Kropf-Godfrey, *A Kafir-English Dictionary* (Lovedale 1915).
Janet Hodgson, *The God of the Xhosa* (Cape Town 1982).
Janet Hodgson, *Ntsikana's Great Hymn* (Cape Town 1980).
T. Soga, *Journal and Selected Writings* (Cape Town 1983).
Xhosa music
D. Dargie, *Xhosa Music* (Cape Town 1988).
Catholic Missions to the Xhosa
W. E. Brown, *The Catholic Church in South Africa* (London 1960).
M. Dischl, *Transkei for Christ*, publ. author, Umtata, 1982.
Lumko Institute
The Lumko Series of Publications: Training for Community Ministries (Various Titles): Lumko, Germiston.
The Lumko Music Tape Series (Church and Traditional Music) (Lumko Marimba Xylophones are built by Bethlehem Brother Kurt Huwiler, Umtata).

Notes

1. Prof. E. G. Parrinder, 'Music in West African Churches', in *African Music*, Vol. 1, No. 3, 1956.
2. Hugh Tracey, 'The Future of Music in Basutoland', in *African Music*, Vol. 2, No. 2, 1959.

PART III

Ritual Music and Cultural Codes

Ruth M. Stone

Sound and Rhythm in Corporate Ritual in Arabia

THE WAYS that people corporately create ritual to express their beliefs in the supernatural reflect both ancient practices and modern adaptations. The Muslims of Arabia, for example, have long performed the call to prayer even though loud speakers now amplify the sound from many mosques. As we explore how Muslim Arabs interpret the call to prayer, we also find that they do not conceive of it as music in the way that we in the West might conceive of it. Furthermore, though the call to prayer is performed five times a day, the way time is ordered for these prayer times is fundamentally different from clock time. The present essay explores religious performance in the prayer call and other Islamic religious rituals of Eastern Arabia in order to provide an understanding of both the sounds and the temporal dimensions of this expression in the present-day context.[1]

The eastern coast of Saudi Arabia presents a fascinating case study of corporate ritual. Rarely can be found in one place so many people of varying nationalities engaged in transforming the landscape so dramatically at one time. The Saudi Arabis are embracing music of the West by buying cassettes and simultaneously isolating that music by restricting it to private arenas. Modern sound-amplification equipment carries the centuries-old call to prayer across the landscape, and television shows prayers from one part of the country to people in another part as a result of modern developments. The corporate Islamic ritual has been largely compartmentalised from modern developments and still reflects important patterns of vocal production and temporal conceptions that have long persisted.

73

For the Arab then, the fundamental sound of corporate ritual centres on the prayer call and prayer. Basic time flow derives from Islam and its observances, and prayer time is fundamental to faith and thus to living life. In a nation that gave birth to Islam, careful observance of this practice is considered a vital, national priority. The king sets an example to his subjects through his personal observance and practice, which the media reports.

The setting of this discussion is ritual as performed in an oil community in the Eastern Province in Arabia. Before the discovery of oil, the east coast of Arabia hosted invaders and guests: the Summerians around 2,000 BC, the Turks until after World War I, and the East Africans, Persians, and Indians brought by the Arabic sailing ships until recent years. When the Americans arrived to explore for oil in the early 1930s, they found several small fishing and pearl diving communities along the Arabian Gulf coast, populated largely by Shi'ite Muslims. In the nearby desert, Bedouin herders travelled with sheep and camels in search of grazing areas and water.

The oil community grew most dramatically in the late 1970s. Families, arriving on the company chartered Boeing 747 that came twice a week from the United States, overflowed into a caravan site of 900 units outside the main camp and were sent to stay in local hotels until housing could be built to accommodate the boom.

Today the modern oil community is home to some 30,000 expatriates and Saudi Arabs though it is still referred to as a 'camp'. The fenced community with several high rise office buildings, a hospital, and two elementary schools, bakery, and ice plant is only a few miles from the two linked towns of Al-Khobar and Ad-Damman. Both of these towns have now grown to several hundred thousand people, each including numerous expatriates as well. Oil is the focal resource and much of the other industry flourishes as a result of vast quantities of oil-generated income. The landscape is that of arid desert edging the Arabian Gulf where rain is slight and temperatures in summer scorching. Drinking water is desalinated and only occasional oases with groves of date palms break the expanse of desert for hundreds of miles. In the last few years the community has decreased: the caravan site is empty and houses in the 'main camp' are being emptied as moving companies pack up many of the inhabitants. People experienced in the oil business cite such sharp rises and falls as typical and today a community of over fifty nationalities includes many Saudi Arabs as well.

The call to prayer punctuates all of life in Arabia, including the oil community, five times a day at dawn, noon, afternoon, sunset, and evening. As the *muezzin* chants from the tower of the mosque, his electronically amplified voice can be heard for long distances, and the calls from neighbouring mosques compete for attention from the faithful. Shopkeepers close their shops hurriedly as customers linger in the streets to wait for reopening some twenty minutes later. Oil company employees need no permission to leave their work to go to the prayer shelter (*masala*) in or near their building and pray. The groups of assembled Muslims, whether in mosques or on the median strip of a busy shopping street, chant prayers in alternation with a leader. As they chant, they alternately stand and prostrate themselves on the ground. Life pauses for prayer, and everyone, regardless of religion, notices this pause.

For the Arabs, the call to prayer (*adhan*) literally means 'hearing' or 'proclamation'. Because of the religious text, Muslims do not consider the call to prayer to be music, for music implies songs with secular texts. Furthermore, as Kristina Nelson has maintained for the recitation of the Qur'an, the call to prayer 'goes beyond euphony: the significance of the revelation is carried as much by the sound as by its semantic information'.[2] Though ethnomusicologists might consider the call to prayer, and the chanted prayers which the gathered group performs, music, because of sustained and rhythmically patterned tones, the Arabs separate these two forms from the *musiqa* (music) that contains texts which comment on things of the secular world.[3] The call to prayer is a regular form of sound art that is at the very core of Islamic life and is heard throughout the Middle East.

The sounding of *adhan* rhythmically punctuates life with continuing regularity. Integrated with the positions of the sun, the prayer times do not, nevertheless, appear to be conceived in a linear manner. Pierre Bordieu, French sociologist, who has worked among Muslims in Morocco, explains that

'The islands of time which are defined by these landmarks are not apprehended as segments of a continuous line, but rather as so many self-enclosed units. . . . Each of the temporal units is an indivisible block juxtaposed to the other.'[4]

These islands do not remain apart from modern time reckoning, for prayer time and clock time intertwine. Saudi Arabia, though spanning the land area of three times zones, operates within a single clock time-zone. Prayer times, however, are tied to the sun positions. On 12 June 1986 the English-language daily *Arab News* lists dawn prayer time (*fajr*) as 4:08 a.m. at Mecca in the west, and 3:100 a.m. at Dammam in the east. The local newspapers publish prayer times daily, for not only do they vary in different regions, but they shift with the seasons and changing sunrise and sunset. In this way, co-ordination of commerce and everyday life on a large scale is attempted, though the connection to clock time remains approximate.

The pause in regular activity, which prayer time engenders, is experienced even by television viewers, for at prayer time the regular programming stops and a sign is projected which reads, 'Prayer Intermission'. Some stations then broadcast the performance of prayers. One station, for example, shows the prayers from the mosque in Mecca, the major holy city. This broadcast is particularly interesting because the non-Muslim, who would not ordinarily be allowed to enter the mosque, is shown this centre through the power of television.

Just as the call to prayer punctuates the day, the period of Ramadan marks the year. Ramadan, a month in the lunar Hijra calandar of the Arabs, brings a change to life. During this period, faithful Muslims refrain from eating or drinking anything from dawn to sunset. Prayer times are extended and in some mosques sunset prayer may even continue into the evening prayer time.

Ramadan is determined to begin when the authorities agree that the sliver of new moon has been sighted by reliable witnesses. Announcements go out asking people to report if they have sighted the moon. The authorities determine locally whether to declare Ramadan to have begun or ended. In earlier times, and in some places yet today, the breaking of the Ramadan fast is announced by a canon shot at sunset. While that sound is eagerly awaited each night, it is particularly anticipated at the end of the month. The sighting of the moon and the beginning and end of Ramadan are more co-incidental than sequential in nature, more mosaic by placement than sequential by cause and effect.

This unusual month of Ramadan also brings a fascinating reversal in the conception of night and day. Because the Muslims fast during the day, they often try to sleep as much as is possible within limits of their work requirements. At the oil company, during this month, all workers start at 6 a.m. instead of the usual 7 a.m. Muslim workers, however, can leave work for the day at 12 noon. Similarly, stores open from 9 a.m. to 12 noon and close until after the evening prayers. They then remain open from 9 p.m. until midnight or later.

During Ramadan, the world comes to life at sunset. Electric lights decorate the homes and stores, and life takes on a festive air. The evening meal is referred to as breakfast. The food is lavish and family and friends gather to share visits and gifts. In a cartoon[5] that appeared during Ramadan, a man in the traditional *thobe* (gown) and *ghoutra* (headdress) staggers under a load of packages he is carrying. He meets a friend who asks, 'Are you hosting a party?' 'No', he responds, 'Just preparing for breakfast.'

Following the food, live music and dance often begin. Even television broadcasts programmes of dance and instrumental music. People explain the music as the result of a longing for times past and a desire to recreate that past. As the dawn nears, people may or may not sleep before they eat a meal to sustain them through the next day of fasting.

Ramadan brings other reversals. Many prisoners receive royal pardons. Beggars receive special help in their poverty as people give *zakat* (alms) in observance of Islam. That people might take advantage of this generosity is expressed in a cartoon which shows two beggars sitting on a street corner below a sign which reads, 'On the Occasion of Gracious Ramadan—Diners Club—American Express—Visa cards accepted to facilitate your charities'.

While the reversal of time may have been somewhat easier to accomplish in smaller nomadic and oasis communities, within a modern industrial complex problems may surface. Feasting requires extra time for shopping and buying special foods and pastries. People who must do their shopping later in the evenings, are compelled to go to work an hour earlier than usual. Merrymaking and partying in the evening take their toll on the workers. The market life adheres to the reversal while the office tries to fit to a western clock time plan. As the month progresses, people show signs of fatigue. The exhilaration of making music together, and of dancing the old dances often wins out as late festivities continue in counterpoint to both office clock time and religious ritual.

The followers of Islam are required to make the *haj*, or pilgrimage to the holy city of Mecca at least once during a lifetime. After Ramadan and for the several months before the *haj* holiday, pilgrims from around the world converge on Mecca. People come by boat, plane, car, and by motorcycle. They come with goods to trade and sell-carpets, spices, manufactured goods. Even those people not making the pilgrimage are kept informed by the mass media of the progress of arrivals. A news story tells that in 1986 only 29,000 pilgrims came from Indonesia, down 9,000 from the previous year. The arrival statistics at the Jeddah airport, the world's most spacious, are daily news items. Thus, for the residents in this Eastern Province community, the pilgrimage season is another annual occurrence in their lives. Some make the pilgrimage themselves from within the country. Others only know of its progress from television or newspaper reports; they make the journey in their minds.

The season of many weddings begins in the month which follows Ramadan and continues up to the pilgrimage. Aside from Ramadan or other holiday performances, the single occasion for traditional music among Saudi Arabs is the wedding. Weddings are held in large receptions halls, often located in hotels, and traditional music bands accompany dance at separate parties for men and for women. A women's band will sing and play frame drums and two-headed cylindrical drums for the women's reception and a group of male musicians will entertain the men's group.

Compared to the performances connected with Islam, traditional Arabic music performance is rare because Muslims question its moral value. A man once recalled wistfully how he, as a young boy, had schemed to obtain an *ud* (lute), only to have his father order him to get rid of the instrument or leave the house.

Musical experiences, which in the West would be public performances, are required by restrictions of Islamic religious observance to be more or less private. What elsewhere would be outside and open is allowed only as inside behaviour. The semi-private performances, permitted within the confines of the oil camp or other limited access areas, do not occur within the other residential sections of towns.

During my four-year residence in Arabia, there was not a single performance of Arabic traditional music within an open and public setting. One Middle Eastern Cultural Night was staged and tickets were sold to employees for a semi-private dinner and performance of dances, predominantly from countries outside of Arabia. The Arabic Speaking Women's Group also provided several semi-private occasions of Middle Eastern musical performance. They hosted a party on one occasion and hired a women's band known as 'The Destinies' from the oasis of Al-Hasa. At another time they staged a fashion show of five weddings from the Middle East, attended, as were all their events, by women only.

While Ramadan and the Pilgrimage provide yearly highlights for the Muslims, the autumn season with its climax at Christmas is the most active social period for the westerners. Music performances are most frequent at this time. An autumn fair in November features a day with a parade, floats, carnival booths and music sponsored by various groups raises money. The oil company theatre group stages a melodrama with men performing women's roles. Interestingly, reversal also characterises the Christmas programme of Bacstage where the ever popular British pantomimes are presented complete with a small orchestra. Children's stories such as 'Jack and the Beanstalk' form the basic vehicles for the pantomimes in which actors play roles of the opposite sex and add many jokes of sexual innuendo. While day and night reversal predominates in Muslim Ramadan, male and female reversal obtains in the pantomimes in the high time of western music performance. In both cases reversal is associated with the high point in the performance year.

The Community Chorale, comprised of Americans and europeans predominantly, performs three major concerts a year in the autumn, spring and summer. Like the other groups, it must submit texts of its planned programmes to the appropriate company reviewer. Some songs may be deleted for objectionable lyrics.[6] Most often lyrics are deemed objectionable for references to Christian practices.

Private house concerts, even more restricted and open by invitation only, are very popular. A hostess invites her guests to hear music from a small group of musicians and organises her living area to accommodate the audience, often serving a buffet reception following the music. I attended a delightful Twelfth Night concert during the Christmas holidays at which there were about forty people.

Audio and video cassette recordings are particularly popular among local Arabs. That which cannot be performed in public can be experienced from a recording in the privacy of a home. Television broadcast is defined in practice as a semi-private medium. Arabs record and enjoy traditional and popular Middle Eastern music beamed from various television stations around the Gulf, the performances showing varying amounts of conservatism in presentation depending upon the country from which they are broadcast. Since television is viewed in the home, in the company of relatives and close friends, considerable freedom is permitted in programming. Men and women can be shown together. Egyptian soap operas of Middle Eastern life, American situation comedies, and Australian dramas are all acceptable after intimate scenes have been excised.

The oil company maintains several FM radio stations and one television station. The radio stations play country and western, 'easy listening', and classical music respectively. Neither the TV nor radio stations prepare live programmes, and on the radio stations indications of time and place are absent. The music, purchased prepackaged, is often streamlined in a 'muzak'-type wrapper. The Arab appreciates music and dance in private settings or occasionally in semi-private settings as a pleasant reminder of the past that has been left behind so suddenly in the oil boom and wave of religious conservatism. In a parallel way, other expatriates long for music that reminds them of home. In the American's case, the enjoyment of groups that were popular in their youth allows them not only to return 'home' through music but to recapture part of time and their youth in music. Adults in their forties and beyond told me that they would not miss a dance or an opportunity to go to one for it brings back vitality that was once theirs. Music of youth and home appears especially vital for people who sometimes spend year after year in a desert landscape with the anchors of their normal life missing.

In the year cycle, we can see that both Arab and western traditions have a period of intense musical activity. For the westerner, this is the autumn period with Christmas as its climax. For the Saudi Arab this is the period from Ramadan through the *haj* and, figured by the lunar calendar, a period that rotates throughout the Gregorian calendar. Since Saudi sensitivities are most acute to even semi-private music performances during Ramadan, the coincidence of ramadan around Christmas time brings out heightened feelings on all sides.

The Saudi Arab publicly follows the prayer call and observes the mandates of Islam. Privately men and women eagerly buy the same recordings that the American or other expatriates long to obtain. Americans, Filipinos, Koreans, Sudanese, and Yemeni all are attracted and enamoured to a certain extent with the latest popular form of music available. Even as the Arabs patronise the tape shops and buy western goods for their homes, they fiercely protect Islam and avoid vices such as *musiqa* in public.

In a world where wristwatches have been manufactured to help determine the direction of Mecca from any place on the globe, and Prayer Minder NL-6 can produce the prayer times for fifty years in 500 different cities, Islam still requires time reckoning by coincidence and consensus. It is the call to prayer, which remains the core of the sound arts in public life. In private life, a desire for the music and styles of the West continues, separated from the public sector practice of Islamic sound art. Yet there is a kind of continuum of compartments within which music is kept. Television schedules reflect that continuum. Call to prayer or recitations from the Qur'an begin the broadcast day. Later follow entertainment shows such as 'Dallas' or an Egyptian soap opera. The day ends and is enclosed again with religious chant. Thus, the outward public shell of Islamic music begins, ends, and punctuates the day as it shields the more veiled consumption of western music of the trendiest sort.

Notes

1 Many people from a variety of nationalities shared ideas that are incorported into this paper. I feel constrained not to name them here since many still live in the community described and because the local community is sensitive about a number of issues raised here. Field research for this paper was carried out from 1982–1986 in the Eastern Province of Saudi Arabia.

2. Kristina Nelson, *The Art of Reciting the Qur'an* (Austin 1985), p. xiv.

3. Lois Ibsen al Faruqi, *An Annotated Glossary of Arabic Musical Terms* (Westport, Conn. 1981), p. 208.

4. Pierre Bordieu, 'The Attitude of the Algerian Peasant Toward Time', in *Mediterranean Countrymen*, edited by J. Pitt-Rivers (The Hague 1963), p. 59.

5. Cartoons constitute an interesting medium in Arabia, for opinions that are seldom voiced publicly frequently appear in this form.

6. The director pointed out that he favoured singing Latin texts and as the Vivaldi *Gloria* which the group had included in a concert this spring because the difficulty of being understood made these texts less subject to censorship.

Ellen Koskoff

Both In and Between: Women's Musical Roles in Ritual Life

WOMEN'S POSITION in many of the world's religions presents a paradox: on the one hand, codified versions of ritual practices often stress a 'female' or 'feminine' principle, one of equal value and weight, acting in harmony with a 'male' counterpart. In many societies, especially those of Asia, female deities, often highly polarised as all-good or all-evil, have tremendous power equal to or perhaps exceeding that of males. If codified religious systems have the function of interpreting the social and cosmic order, and of providing prescriptions for appropriate social interaction, then it would appear from this tendency to valourise the feminine that women, like men, would, even at the everyday, 'on-the-ground' level of culture, have equal participation in social and ritual life.

Yet, despite this conceptual framework, in the vast majority of cases, women's actual involvement in ritual, especially as music specialists, is severely limited and women's rituals are often described as 'relegated' to the home or as 'peripheral' to the mainstream. Understanding why this is so may lie in examining more of what occupies the space or gap between a culturally constructed, over-arching theory that presents the idealised and generalised concept of male and female—often enacted ritually—and the every-day social reality of women and men, whose relationships and interdependencies are enacted on a daily, often changeable basis. Within this gap lie ideologies that provide frameworks for such interactions; ideologies that are often contradictory to more idealised concepts. This paper explores the notion that women and the music they perform, can be seen as simultaneously 'in' and 'between' various domains and, further, that they derive their power and efficacy precisely from this intermediate position. Using a theory proposed by Sherry Ortner[1] that posits women's role as mediator between nature and culture, I present three case studies that explore the relationship between women, music and power within very different religious and social settings and suggest widely different possibilities for their interaction.[2]

Ortner's view is that all societies construct conceptual categories, 'nature' and 'culture', that are used to separate humans from non-humans. Built into this primary distinction is a value system that places humans, their activities and artifacts ('culture') at a higher level than non-humans ('nature'). 'Thus culture (*i.e.* every culture) at some level of awareness asserts itself to be not only distinct from but superior to nature, and that sense of distinctiveness and superiority rests precisely on the ability to transform—to "socialise" and "culturalise"—nature' (p. 73). Women, as bearers, nurturers and primary socialisers of all children, and yet existing also in the world of 'humans' (*i.e.* properly socialised adults) are seen everywhere as occupying an intermediate position between the two domains, and thus, universally subordinated and devalued.[3]

There has been some criticism of Ortner's work, especially her assertion of the universality of female subordination. Many researchers, although acknowledging that societies universally differentiate (often polarise) male and female and the cultural domains over which they have control, also suggest that value systems placing females in a subordinate position to males are not always present. Societies do exist where males and females may lack access to each other's domains, yet both the sexes and the domains are equally valued. Further, many societies, such as those influenced by Confucianism or native American beliefs, stress harmony between nature and culture and see humans as existing in balance, not in conflict, with non-humans. Finally, Ortner does not address the spirit world, for many, a real place inhabited by dead ancestors, great leaders, ghosts or demons, all of whom can have an effect upon both nature and culture. In fact, the relationship of the mundane world to the spiritual can be seen as analogous to that between culture and nature, and it is here, too that women, in many cultures act as both in and between.

However, it is Ortner's elaboration on the intermediate position of women that is the most suggestive for our purposes. She describes three interpretations of women's intermediacy: (1) where 'intermediate' may have the significance of 'middle status' (*i.e.* women exist on a 'hierarchy of being from culture to nature'; (2) where intermediate may imply 'mediating', that is, synthesising or converting; and (3) where the intermediate position of women carries the implication of 'greater symbolic ambiguity' (pp. 84–85).

From Ortner's perspective, the first interpretation answers her primary question as to the 'whys' of universal female subordination; the third interpretation helps to explain the polarised female symbolism in many world religions (as well as art, law or ritual): 'Feminine symbolism, far more often than masculine symbolism, manifests this propensity toward polarised ambiguity—sometimes utterly exalted, sometimes utterly debased, rarely within the normal range of human possibilities' (p. 86). It is the second interpretation, that of women's position as mediator, that I wish to explore here, for it is this aspect of (universal?) gender ideology that I believe has the most implications for women's musical roles in ritual life.

Ortner sees women's mediating position as essentially that of 'synthesiser' or 'converter' between nature and culture, yet there are other senses of the word 'mediate' that seem to have more relevance to women's ritual roles, for these roles tend to posit women both in and between the everyday world, inhabited by both humans and non-humans, (*i.e.* nature *and* culture) and the divine world of spirits (not addressed by Ortner). Here, the word 'mediate' takes on the sense of 'intercede,' 'intervene,' or 'negotiate' and it is in this sense that I wish to address the issue of women as both in and between.

Music sound and performance also carry the implication of intermediacy, in the same sense as above. Often described as a channel or vehicle that transports humans from one psychological state to another, from the mundane to the spiritual, or from one social status to another, music has power that is believed to be only partially controlled by humans and its use is often limited, especially in ritual contexts, to a few specialists. Thus, like women, it can be seen as existing both in and between, not only 'nature' (*i.e.* uncontrollable sound) and 'culture,' (efficacious sound), but also in and between one social/spiritual state and another. In this 'negotiating' capacity, music and its performance can be useful in communicating with the spirit world, in settling disputes, or in protesting various social actions, such as war or unwanted marriages (see especially Joseph 1980). Music performance can also act to mediate overt antagonisms between the sexes (Gourlay 1975; Basso 1987).

When women perform music, the combined ambiguity of both women and music's symbolic and real position as 'mediators' creates tremendous potential power. Each society attempts to regulate such power (often seen as threatening to the social and sexual order) in its own way and nowhere is this control better manifested than in ritual practice.

Jewish women and music

Among Orthodox Jews, the performance of music is considered a spiritual necessity, yet many of the codified laws of Judaism exclude adult women from overt, public music making.[4] Although many social and religious justifications exist for this, the most important stems from various legal interpretations of a Biblical passage from Solomon's Song of Songs, 'For your voice is sweet and your face beautiful' (Jones 1966, 2:14). Talmudic scholars, in interpreting this passage, fully elaborated upon its sexual implications. Maimonides, for example, interpreted it as follows: 'He who stares even at a woman's little finger with the intention of deriving pleasure from it, is considered as though he had looked at her secret parts. It is forbidden to listen even to the singing of a woman' (5:21:2). Eventually, a large body of literature arose dealing with the issue of *kol ishah* (the voice of a woman—both singing and speaking), which continues today to be regarded as a serious distraction to men. Any situation that would encourage a man to become *ervah* (sexually promiscuous) and might result in his abandoning the true religious purpose of his life, is strictly prohibited. Although the proscription is placed on the man, that is, *he* is not permitted to hear the (by inference, sexually attractive) woman, in reality, adult women simply do not sing (or pray) in the presence of men.

One other factor must be mentioned here as affecting women's ritual activities in Orthodox Judaism. There are 613 commandments, related by law and custom to Orthodox Jewish activities. Although both men and women are expected to adhere to these laws, women are given some freedom (especially during childbearing years) and are exempted from all commandments related to time and place. Thus, for example, many of the laws dictating synagogue prayer at specific times of the day are not followed by most adult females. As caretakers of the home and children, such women must be free to fulfil other commandments that have a higher priority.

The effect of these exemptions, combined with the prohibition against hearing *kol ishah*, effectively prevents (or excuses) women from participating freely with men in many of the public ritual activities of Orthodox Judaism. For example, in Orthodox synagogues men and women are separated from each other during services or other events, such as Sabbath meals or weddings, where the danger of hearing a woman sing or pray exists. Even among Reform Jews, who long ago abandoned many of the older, orthodox practices, women, until recently have been prevented from becoming cantors.[5]

Among Lubavitcher Hasidim ('pious', ultra-orthodox Jews) with whom I worked, one event, the *farbrengen*, highlights the extent to which women are barred from public ritual activity. The *farbrengen* is a gathering that unites the community with its spiritual leader, or Rebbe. During a *farbrengen*, the Rebbe delivers a spiritual message, usually focusing on a specific topical issue affecting the community as a whole. His speaking, which can continue for hours, is punctuated at various intervals with the singing of special para-liturgical songs, called *nigunim*. These are believed to be vehicles for achieving the two emotional states, *simhah* (joy) and *hitlahavut* (enthusiasm) essential for spiritual fulfilment (*devekuth*, or 'adhesion'). The performance of *nigunim*, especially in the presence of the Rebbe, is considered to be one of the most effective ways to achieve *devekuth*, and, as such, is a spiritual necessity, in theory, for all Lubavitchers.

Women who attend *farbrengen* sit in a gallery high above the Rebbe and other males. The gallery is enclosed by sheets of tinted plastic, so that it is difficult to hear the proceedings below. Sitting quietly in the gallery, reading from a book of prayers, or perhaps chatting with friends about family affairs, the women do not sing, nor seem to participate in the events in any way. Their surroundings have effectively removed them physically and visually, as well as spiritually, from the men, the Rebbe, and *nigun* performance.

The women themselves (as opposed to the 'outside' ethnographer) do not see this as evidence of a 'second-class' position. They resent the perception of feminists that their status is measured in terms of 'where they sit in the synagogue' (Lubavitch Foundation 1970, p. 217). Rather, they regard their exemption from many of the commandments and their lack of musical activity as a sign of superiority: 'For to the extent that the *Mitzvahs* [commandments] constitute an exercise in self-discipline for moral advancement . . . it would seem that the Creator has endowed Jewish woman with a greater measure of such natural self-discipline' (p. 220). Judaism, with its strong emphasis on the family unit as the prime locus of spirituality, regards women's position in the home as highly valuable and a powerful counterpart to men's ritual activities in the synagogue.

One of the things that I began to see as fieldwork continued was a certain parallel between the Lubavitcher concept of music as a 'channel' between the mundane and the divine, and the role of woman as mediator between the religious and secular. Lubavitcher women, in a sense, have more freedom than their male counterparts to interact with the outside, non-Lubavitcher environment. Many young, married women work outside the home in shops or as secretaries, often to support their husbands' studies. Most speak English among themselves (many of the men, even those born in the United States, speak Yiddish); some will occasionally read popular magazines, listen to the radio or attend a movie, activities that are usually prohibited for adult males and children. Women see themselves as both part of the Lubavitcher world and as acting to protect their families from the more or less hostile, non-religious world. They are, more than men, cognisant of both worlds and function much of the time negotiating both in and between them.

Further, although all Lubavitchers recognise the effectiveness of *nigun* performance, it is rare to hear older, married women singing, even in the privacy of their homes with no men present. Young girls, before the age of puberty, are frequent singers around the Sabbath table, and, if in attendance at Sabbath services or *farbrengen*, may sit with their fathers (or, more commonly, run about, not paying too close attention to the proceedings) in the lower portion of the synagogue. When a young girl is to marry, her friends prepare a *forshpil*, a large and raucous party filled with much singing and dancing that marks her transition into her true, adult, settled status. From then on, there is usually little music-making, most music performance now regarded as a more or less frivolous activity associated with youth, and *nigun* performance described as 'what the men do.'

It is clear that in the Lubavitcher world, both music and women serve a mediating function. For men, music acts throughout their lives as the vehicle through which they achieve *devekuth*; for women, it serves to mark their transition from one social status to another. Yet, women themselves are mediators, acting on behalf of their families, existing both in the Lubavitcher world and between that and the potentially threatening secular one. Further, females also exist between two other poles: uncontrolled sexuality (*i.e.* unmarried—nature?) and controlled sexuality (*i.e.* married—culture?). Thus, within the context of Orthodox Judaism and Lubavitcher beliefs, ritually important music (*nigun*) must remain within the hands of men, as performance by sexually active females might prove too disruptive.

Female shamans in Korea

In Korea the social position of women has, until recently, suffered under the neo-Confucian philosophical/religious system that entered Korea with the Yi dynasty (1392–1910). Whether or not extreme Confucianist beliefs that saw women's position to men as analogous to that of men to the Gods ever took hold in Korea as they did in China, is still in question, but there is no doubt that similar ideologies continue today to constrain women's social and religious activities.

Kept in relative seclusion, women of the upper castes are to serve males in the home, most importantly, by producing male heirs. Within this social and economic context, however, females frequently develop powerful relationships with each other. Many of their ritual activities are directed toward family and household concerns: the birth of sons, the curing of illness, forecasting the marriage of a daughter, appeasing dead souls, removing evil spirits, and so on. Many household and village rituals, often described by male Koreans and by western religious scholars as 'folk rituals', as opposed to 'Confucianism'—the official, written philosophical system of males—are controlled by women shamans (*mudang*) and are carried out primarily on behalf of other women and families.[6]

Shamanism has been an integral part of Korean ritual life for centuries and has always been in the hands of women, who today represent about 95 per cent of the total number of shamans. Male shamans (*paksu mudang*), considered to be marginal males, will dress in female ritual costume when performing (Harvey 1980, p. 52, n. 1). Shamans are of two types: those, primarily from the North, whose role is hereditary, and those, from the South, who are 'chosen' by spirits as ritual specialists.[7] The term, *mudang* (shaman) is used to denote the generalised role, whereas *mansin* (literally, 'ten thousand spirits') refers specifically to the chosen, professional shaman who performs *kuts*.

A *kut* is a musico-dramatic ritual called by a *mansin* who mediates between a client, having paid for her services, and various spirits who enter and speak from her body during trance. *Kuts* can be held for individual men or women at household shrines, or for an entire village or city at a larger, public shrine, thus uniting families under one concern, such as the consecration of a new building or a local drought.

Men appear to have no interest in *kuts*, and will sit passively during a performance, even if it has been called on their behalf. During a *kut*, the *mansin* acts in ways that are antithetical to prevailing notions of proper behaviour for women, both in the context of a *kut*—where she may speak directly, often with considerable anger, and dance wildly to the accompanying music—as well as in the larger social context of her town or village—where she is often unmarried and considered to have an especially low social status. If married, her status is considered to be higher than that of her husband, who frequently acts as her assistant during a *kut*, performing various musical instruments. The relationship of a *mansin* to her husband thus further defies Korean notions of gender relations.

Becoming a *mansin* involves a three-stage process: spirit appearance, 'spirit sickness' (*sinbyŏng*) and an initiation *kut*. Often 'summoned' by spirits when quite young, a future *mansin* begins to act 'strangely', becoming depressed, perhaps sexually active, or exhibiting symptoms of mental illness.

When the 'spirit sickness' begins, a family will take the child to the local, established *mansin* to determine whether or not this is truly a forecast of the girl's status as shaman, or simply mental illness. When it is established that the girl is to become a *mansin*, she is apprenticed to the older shaman and learns the songs, dances and pantheon of spirits that she will later invoke during *kuts*. At the completion of this spiritual training, an initiatory *kut* is held on her behalf, where she demonstrates her ability to contact the spirit world during trance, and, having been successful, she moves into her new social and ritual role.[8]

Kuts also fall into three categories that are distinguished by length and by the type of female who is in control: (1) the *pison*, lasting an hour or so, can be performed by an ordinary housewife as well as a shaman; (2) the *p'udakkori*, lasting three or four hours is often conducted by a fortuneteller or shaman; and (3) the greater *kut*, which often lasts several days and is performed only by a shaman (Huhm 1980, pp. 11–12). During the greater *kut*, a series of spirits are summoned on behalf of the client, including great male leaders of past Korean dynasties, various male and female ancestors of the client's family, and martial spirits used to drive away the evil demons or ghosts inhabiting a person who is ill or an unfortunate household. Trance is induced by performance on various musical instruments, including a double-headed, hour-glass drum, flute, gong, one-stringed fiddle, and a large wand upon which are fastened five to nine jingle bells (Covell 1983, pp. 40–41). While in trance, the *mansin*, may wield a knife, a tri-pointed spear, and/or a halberd—a crescent-shaped axe used to slice through the chest of an offending spirit.

The ritual power of the *mansin* is not questioned. In total control of both the trance-inducing music and the 'ten thousand spirits', in whose voices she speaks, her actions can decide the fate of a childless couple or the auspiciousness of a new downtown auditorium. Further, although not officially recognised by the male dominated Confucian and Buddhist ritual/political hierarchies, the power of the *mansin* and the efficacy of *kut* are nevertheless regarded as crucial to the running of the household and continue to be called today on a regular basis.

Thus, unlike the Orthodox Jewish women above, Korean *mansin* are the main conduits to the spirit world. As women with special powers, their ritual position is higher than that of Jewish women, in that they have sole access to the spirit world that decides the affairs of family and household. They are, in a sense, analogous to *nigun*, in that they act to mediate on behalf of humans, intervening, placating and negotiating in a direct way with the spirits who decide the outcome of everyday human actions. Yet, unlike Jewish women, their social and official religious status is low and families whose children exhibit early signs of 'spirit sickness' often hide in fear and embarrassment, only reluctantly acknowledging their child's potential power.

Iroquois women's rites

Among the Iroquois, women have traditionally held positions of great power and prestige.[9] Their social structure, often referred to erroneously as a 'matriarchy', implying women's control and authority over men, is matrilineal, that is, descent is reckoned through the mother. Upon meeting someone for the first time, the question, 'Who is your mother?' establishes the person within a matrilineal-extended family, a clan (families of the mother's siblings), a moiety ('half' or 'side'), a tribe, and many other familial, ritual and political networks (Shimony 1961; Allen 1986). Within this framework, women as well as men are seen as equally important and valuable to the balance of life, and although they each control specific ritual, social and economic domains, no one domain is valued over the other, both seen as necessary and complementary.

Today, the Iroquois are a league of six native tribes (Mohawk, Seneca, Onondaga, Oneida, Cayuga and, an adopted tribe, the Tuscorora), many of whom live at the Six Nations Reserve near Brantford, Ontario. About one-third of the current population follow the teachings of the Seneca prophet, Handsome Lake (d. 1799), who founded the Longhouse religion in the late eighteenth century, a time of tremendous social and political upheaval. Deceived by both the British and American governments, the Iroquois not only lost much of their land and hunting rights after the Revolution, but also their own autonomous political power. Further, white notions of male control over social, political and economic institutions (patriarchy) and of basic citizenship, reckoned in European social organisation through the father (patriliny), came into conflict with basic native notions of family and society. During this period of upheaval, many Iroquois suffered from alcoholism, which contributed greatly to other social problems such as wife and child abuse. It was within this social context that the Seneca prophet, Handsome Lake, arose with his messages of individual and social reform. Now representing a conservative element at the Six Nations Reserve, the followers of Handsome Lake continue to practise the older, more traditional rituals in the face of widespread acculturation among their Christian colleagues (Shimony 1961).

The Code of Handsome Lake (*Kaiwiyoh*) is a collection of stories, myths, rules of conduct and prescriptions for behaviour that are believed to have been revealed to the prophet by four spirit-messengers sent by the creator.

It combines elements of traditional (pre-contact) practices and beliefs with Christian (European) ideals, which initially allowed its followers to return to more traditional ways, thus restoring some of their former dignity and power, while at the same time subtly changing the relationships between the sexes that would have implications for future ritual and social life.

For example, in pre-contact times, men generally hunted and conducted large-scale inter-tribal wars, which removed them from the local communities, while women assumed control over agriculture (including growing and exchanging food) as well as tribal concerns, as the men were frequently away for great periods of time. One of the women's most important duties was the election of a 'peace chief', a member of an hereditary council that was responsible for tribal governance. (Shimony 1980, p. 247). Chief's 'matrons' were responsible for choosing a new peace chief and could also impeach a chief if his actions were disruptive to tribal life. In 1924 the Canadian government insisted that the Iroquois choose members of the council by general election (a point of contention and protest even to this day), and as a result of this intervention, the power of both the chief and chief's matrons diminished.

Further, when hunting lands were taken from the Iroquois, the entire economic structure was upset. Handsome Lake specifically addressed this problem in his Code, suggesting that male Iroquois now adapt to three things that white men (referred to as 'our younger brothers') did that were 'right to follow': cultivate and harvest food, keep cattle, and build 'warm and fine appearing' (*i.e.* European style) housing (Parker 1913, p. 38, Section 25). Effectively, the Code prescribed changing the entire social structure of the Iroquois from a horticultural society, where women had tremendous political and economic power, to an agrarian one, where the control of food production and distribution now fell to both men and women, and where women's autonomy decreased (O'Kelly and Carney 1986, p. 50).

Although some contemporary Iroquois remain farmers, most travel to nearby cities, such as Brantford, Toronto, Niagara Falls or Buffalo, New York, for work, so the former agricultural cycle that regulated work and marked the year into periods associated with planting and harvesting, no longer has the same social meaning. However, as today's Iroquois move farther away from their traditional economic way of life, the importance of Longhouse rituals has grown, and within the Longhouse religion the role of women has taken on a dignity and power reminiscent of past times. Women are now prominent as 'faithkeepers' or 'deaconesses', and their duties include scheduling and conducting women's rituals and ceremonies as well as counselling or settling quarrels (Shimony 1980, pp. 254–256).

Four Longhouse congregations exist today at the Six Nations Reserve. According to Shimony, the roles of men and women are highlighted both in the spacial layout of the Longhouse itself and in the division of the rituals into men's and women's observances:

'Members say that they enter by the men's or women's door and sit on the men's or women's side. During the rites themselves, action is reciprocal between the two domains, and much of the service consists of dialogue between the opposing units. Thus, on the whole, a balance is struck, and the efficacy of a ceremony depends upon the combined efforts of whatever divisions are at play (1980, pp. 250–251).

One ritual, not part of the agricultural cycle, the *Ohgi'we*, or Feast of the Dead, highlights the powerful position of women in Iroquois society.[10] During the *Ohgi'we*, the spirits of dead ancestors are contacted and placated to insure harmony and balance in the earthly realm. *Ohgi'we* also acts as a healing ceremony to cure 'ghost sickness' or possession. Women are seen as the main channels through which the spirit word is contacted and the *Ohgi'we* takes place on the woman's side of the Longhouse. Yet, although women schedule and execute these ceremonies, and are the main dancers, in traditional complementary fashion, men are also involved in important ritual roles, mainly as assistant drummers and singers, and both sexes must be present for the ceremony to be effective.

Summary and conclusions

When we compare the social and ritual position of Iroquois women with their Jewish and Korean counterparts described above, what is most apparent is the acknowledgment in Iroquois society—but not in traditional Orthodox Judaism or Confucianism—of the value and power inherent in both the women and their music, a power that is perhaps feared, but ultimately respected. The value accorded Iroquois women of today may stem from earlier times, when they had considerable economic and political control, yet even though their real power has diminished, their position in the traditional social and belief system as complementary counterparts to the male has not. In this position, they have equal access to ritual music and ceremony, performing their own songs and dances in their own side of the Longhouse, the centre of ritual life. Here, combining the power of women with that of music is not threatening, but rather seen as a necessary balance to male ritual activity.

From the above examples, it is clear that there is a wide range of social and religious contexts where women and music interact in a variety of ways. The position of women as more or less 'in' and 'between' natural, cultural and spiritual domains is ultimately related to a society's notions of gender, power and value that regulate all aspects of life. Understanding women's ritual and ceremonial roles is impossible unless we see women, men and ritual as interacting within the larger social, economic and political world.

Notes

1. 'Is Female to Male as Nature is to Culture', in *Women, Culture and Society*, ed. M. Z. Rosaldo and L. Lamphere (Stanford 1974).

2. For an excellent discussion of the recent literature on changing roles for women in Christian ritual and liturgy, I refer the reader to Anne Barstow Driver's Review essay in *Signs* 1976.

3. See also Chodorow 1974 for a discussion of the implications of women as primary socialisers, and Strathern 1972 for a further analysis of the position of women as 'in between'.

4. See Koskoff 1976 and 1987 for a fuller discussion of women's music-making in Orthodox Judaism.

5. See Slobin, in press, for an excellent discussion of recent changes.

6. For a fuller, cross-cultural treatment of shamanism, see the classic studies by Eliade 1964 and I. M. Lewis 1971, 1986. See also Rouget 1985 for a discussion of music and trance. For a description of shamanism in Korea, see especially Kendall 1985 and Harvey 1980.

7. Many chosen, 'professional' shamans migrated from North to South Korea during the Korean War (1950–53) and much ritual activity takes place today in and around the Seoul area.

8. Some Western scholars (especially Harvey 1980) have suggested that the extreme sexual repression of Korean women, and their general lack of access to positions of power or authority, can account for the rather high instance of 'spirit sickness' and female shamanism in Korea, where, in trance, a *mansin* can act freely in an aggressive or highly sexual manner.

9. See Shimony 1980, 1961, Fenton 1951, and Tooker 1986 for excellent discussions of the Iroquois.

10. See Shimony 1980 and Fenton and Kurath 1951/1985 for excellent descriptions of this ceremony.

Sue Carole DeVale

Power and Meaning in Musical Instruments[1]

POWER AND meaning are invested in musical instruments throughout the world. They are ascribed to musical instruments essential to the efficacy of rituals of all kinds, from those ensuring fertility to those of royal courts.[2] In construction, the instruments range from the deceptively simple, such as a whittled bullroarer, to the extremely complex, such as a forged bronze gong. Power in musical instruments resides in the spirits believed to be embodied within them or working through them; it often emanates from their music, their very sound.

The meaning of a musical instrument may be signified externally in its design, construction and care, or lie in the internal domain of cultural understanding. In many cultures of the world, no clear line separates the sacred and the secular. Thus meaning in musical instruments often lies along a physical-metaphysical continuum from the earthly to the divine.

The purpose of this paper is to provide material for reflection on the essential spiritual role of musical instruments in the life of mankind. First, it will investigate the nature of the spiritual presence in musical instruments and then the powers ascribed to them. Secondly, it will explicate the ways in which musical instruments embody cultural concepts, ultimately capable of manifesting the union of the microcosmos and the macrocosmos; *i.e.* the human and the spirit worlds.[3]

The spiritual presence in musical instruments

The spiritual presence in musical instruments arises from myriad religions: forms of animism, so-called ancestor worship, or theism, as well as syncretic belief systems. The spirits, normally beneficent, may be those of sacred raw materials, animals or environmental spirits, guardians or geniuses; they may be ancestors, saints, gods or goddesses. All the instruments of a culture, or a specific kind of instrument such as drums, may be manifestations of the same spirit. Or, an instrument, or even an entire ensemble, may have its own particular spirit. Musical instruments (or, more properly, their spirits) are often acknowledged and honoured with rituals and ritual procedures which may occur at various stages in the life-cycle of the instruments from before construction to after their useful life.[4] A few examples will be offered to illustrate the range of spirits manifested in musical instruments and some of the rituals which pay tribute to them.

Drums of the Akan peoples of Ghana are regarded as 'the repositories of the spirit of *Tweneboa Kadua*', the sacred tree from which they are made; specific rituals honour that spirit as well as the ancestors associated with the drums.[5] Before the tree is cut down to make a drum, it is offered libations, asking the tree spirit to enter the drum that will be made from it. After the drums are completed, the spirit of the tree continues to be honoured and thus Akan drums share in the libations and sacrifices of festivals for which their music is essential. Before most performances, state drummers, especially those of talking drums,[6] offer a brief libation to *Tweneboa Kadua* and to the ancestor drummers. Performances on the *atumpan*, the principal talking drum of the Akan, begin with a special drum prelude called 'The Awakening', during which the spirit of each part of a drum is invoked, including not only that of *Tweneboa Kadua*, but all the other trees and bark used in the drum, even that of the elephant who gave his ear to become the drumhead.

In Java and Bali, Indonesia, *gamelan* orchestras with from seven to seventy instruments, primarily bronze gongs and metallophones (xylophones with metal keys), have traditionally been essential to religious rites and the accompaniment of dance, as well as for concert music. In Central Java, a gamelan is believed to have its own personal guardian spirit or spirit presence who resides in the largest hanging gong (*gong ageng*).[7] A gamelan is usually given a proper name in a special naming ceremony followed by a *slametan*, a community ritual feast. In addition, incense and flowers, and sometimes a cooked chicken, are offered to the *gong ageng* during performances. Other common practices show respect for the gamelan; *e.g.* no musician sits higher than the *gong ageng* nor enters the

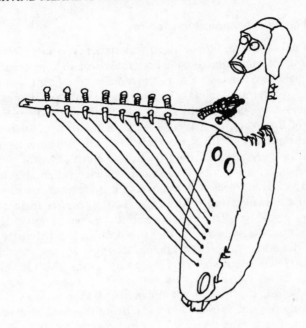

Figure 1: *Ngombi*, generalised example

area enclosed by the gamelan's instruments with his shoes on.[8] Sacred gamelans may be given ritual washings before they are used; they are often stored in their own special houses or buildings when they are not in use, sometimes they are even played in them.

Among the Newar of Nepal, most musical instruments are considered to be manifestations of the same god: *Nasa:dya:*, the god of music.[9] Near the end of most performances, the music stops and members of the audience hold a *Nasa:dya: Puja*, a ritual to honour the instruments, along with books of music notation and texts, with a variety of offerings including flowers, incense and money.

Instruments may be manifestations of goddesses or saints like the *ngombi*, the eight-string harp essential to Fang Bwiti ritual in Gabon.[10] In its voice and body, the *ngombi* is believed to be Nyingwan Mbege, the Sister of God (or the Blessed Virgin in the Christianised versions), and is often carved or sculpted with an image of her face and head (as in Fig. 1).[11] As the Sister of God, the harp is the power of the night, her symbol is the moon; she must not be exposed to the light of the male power of day, the sun. Thus, at the end of the all night Bwiti ceremonies, four 'exit songs' are sung for the harp while it is danced in procession from the chapel to its own, sacred light-tight storage chamber at the end of the village.[12]

There are only a very few reported cases of musical instruments thought to have malevolent spirits. In two known to me, they are cases in which a normally beneficent spirit becomes temporarily malicious, primarily as the consequence of the omission of a prescribed ritual in its honour. This may be a reason why few cases have been reported: such rituals are rarely omitted because of dire consequences.

Kakraba Lobi, a Ghanaian xylophone musician and maker, reported to me his experience with the spirit of the particular tree that was embodied in a xylophone. He had been in such a hurry to make a xylophone for a customer that he omitted the offering to the spirit of the tree before he cut it down. He proceeded to complete the instrument and then immediately became seriously ill with edema, upon which medical science, including hospitalisation, had apparently no effect. He was cured soon after he returned to the tree's stump, placed a food offering at its base and apologised with prayers.

The consequence of forgetting to present regular ritual offerings to a particular sacred Javanese gong is of quite a different nature. '*K. K. Sima*' ('Most Venerable Tiger'), is one of two revered gongs in a sacred gamelan known as '*K. K. Mahesa Ganggang*' ('Most Venerable Fighting Buffalo'), whose instruments are tuned to a sacred three-tone scale. Kunst reports that the caretakers of the gamelan believe that if they fail to take all possible care of it and, especially if they forget to bring the gong the regularly prescribed offerings of flowers and incense, that they will 'suddenly come face to face with a tiger'.[13]

Power in musical instruments

The power invested in musical instruments is of wide range. It may be preventative or curative for both the human body and the human soul, or provide wealth, fertility and other blessings. It may be essential to subsistence or to increase human physical strength. An instrument may serve as a vehicle for communication between the world of the living and that of the ancestors and gods, the seen and the unseen. The magical power of musical instruments may be accumulable by the owner of the instruments. While the power of an instrument usually emanates from its sound or music, this is not always the case; sometimes an instrument will continue to have a spiritual function after it is no longer played, or even be assigned a new religious function which it didn't have while it was playable.

In Java, a variety of powers are ascribed to gamelan, particularly those with bronze instruments. The forging of bronze, like certain other metals, is associated with fire and the power of vulcanoes and gods. In Central Java, gamelans are thought to have a kind of charismatic or magical power, called *kasektén*, which may be accumulated by the owner. Consequently, it is an old tradition in Java for the princes and rulers to own many gamelans as well as other powerful *pusaka* (sacred heirlooms) items such as *krisses* (daggers), spears and state carriages.[14] In Central Javanese villages, the sound of certain gamelans is believed to have the power to bring rain necessary for rice agriculture. The sacred gamelan, *goong renteng*, belonging to the Sundanese (West Javanese) village of Lebakwangi, is played only on official occasions to ritually purify the village or otherwise safeguard it from possible misfortune and harm.[15] Gamelan music is essential to efficacy of *wayang kulit* (shadow puppet plays) and *wayang golek* (rod puppets of Sunda) which may be performed ritually in such as rites of passage.

The myths of the Dan of the Ivory Coast credit animals and bush spirits with the invention of their musical instruments.[16] The Dan believe that spirits are especially fond of music and thus help musicians play with great energy. In addition to being pleasurable, music is thought to impart physical strength, especially for fatiguing or dangerous activities like agriculture, building houses, warfare and hunting. For example, a special harp, the *ko*, is associated with hunters and taken with them during a hunt.[17] Before tracking game, the hunters sing and dance to gather strength and courage, accompanied by the harpist. The Dan further believe the sound of the harp ensures them a more successful hunt by improving their aim and by giving them power over the guardian spirits of animals.

Faith in the power of musical instruments to assist and affect spirit possession and exorcism is widespread in Africa, South and Southeast Asia. An African case will serve as an example. The Shona of Zimbabwe believe that one must remember the family ancestor spirits (*vadzimu*) and honour their moral values and, that they, in turn, will protect the living.[18] When misfortunes occur, such as prolonged illness, a death in the family or even crop failure, they believe the ancestor spirits were offended in some way. The *bira* is an all-night ceremony in which common ancestor spirits are invoked by family members to enter and be consulted by a spirit medium who will help diagnose the cause of the misfortune. The nucleus of the music for the *bira*, is provided by the *mbira dzavadzimu*, a lamellaphone often with twenty-two keys spanning a four-octave range (Fig. 2).[19] Berliner relates:

Figure 2: *Mbira dzavadzimu*, without gourd resonator

'A well-known mbira player who performed for a powerful medium told me, "The mbira is not just an instrument to us. It is like your Bible. . . . It is the way in which we pray to God." In the context of the *bira*, the people believe the mbira to have the power to project its sound into the heavens, bridging the world of the living and the world of the spirits and thereby attracting the attention of the ancestors. In the hands of skillful musicians the mbira is able to draw spirits to earth to possess mediums. At the *bira*, the members of the mbira ensemble are responsible for the possession of the spirit medium or mediums. Their music, moreover, places other villagers in a meditative state and inspires their tireless participation in the dancing, clapping, and singing which accompany the mbira music throughout the evening.'[20]

As the voice of the Sister of God, the Fang Bwiti *ngombi*, the harp mentioned above, is thought to have the power to drive evil spirits out of the chapel making it possible for the ancestors to enter.[21] The music of the harp is believed to be that played by the dead in the afterworld, or the angels in heaven in the Christianised forms of Bwiti. The harp is regarded as the primary path of intercommunication between the worlds of the seen and the unseen; the eight strings, like the eight sacred trees, are considered to be locales for sending and receiving messages between them. The harp carries the prayers of the Bwiti to the ancestors and gods and returns their blessings.

The personal spirits of instruments may be trusted to have such magical power that they are the object of prayers. '*Kyai Kangjeng Nagawilaga*' ('Most Venerable Fighting Serpent'), one of the two sacred *gamelan sekati* in the Kraton Yogyakarta, a Central Javanese court, is ascribed such power, and the people of the city seek help from the spirit in resolving problems in their lives.[22] During *Sekaten* week, the week preceding Mohammed's birthday, the two *gamelan sekati* are played every day in alternation at approximately half-hour intervals.[23] During the periods when 'K. K. Nagawilaga' is not being played, a steady stream of people hand flower petals and incense wrapped in banana leaves to a religious official, whispering their request in his ear. The official carries them to the gamelan, placing the petals inside the hollow back of the *gong ageng* and setting the incense in a clay pot to burn. Fanning the incense, he quietly passes on the request to the gamelan's spirit via the *gong ageng*.

Sometimes instruments are considered to have power or a spiritual function even after their useful life as instruments of music. A large *glong* drum, one of an incomplete ensemble that is no longer played by the northern Dan of the Ivory Coast, is essential to ancestor worship and serves as a kind of medium for communication with them.[24] It is offered prayers and sacrifices by the chief before invoking the ancestors, who were once performers of these drums, to bless the community and bring it good fortune, riches and many children.

Meaning in musical instruments

In their meaning, musical instruments embody concepts that link the visual, aural, social and spiritual realms of culture. Symbolism may inform the naming of parts of an instrument and aesthetic parallels may exist between instrument design and other arts. Musical instruments are commonly anthropomorphised and zoomorphised. This can be observed at many levels from the carving, sculpting or decoration of instruments with human or animal forms to the naming of their parts. For example, in the West, guitars and harps are said to have 'necks', violins and lutes also have 'bellies', and drums have 'heads'.

The parts of instruments: social and religious concepts

The names of instrument parts may reflect human and animal sounds and attributes, as well as deeper social and religious concepts. African harps will serve as examples.

Two sets of names are reported for the strings of a family of three harps, *galdama*, *direndana* and *kolo*, used by the Kotoko southeast of Lake Chad.[25] Although the harpists are men, the harps are the primary instruments in exorcism rituals only for women. The three harps, with overlapping ranges, each have five strings. In one interpretation, from lowest to highest, they are called: (1) *bo*, elephant scream, *i.e.*, something very strong; (2) *wanda*, something of no value; (3) *direndana*, middle, one who gives justice; (4) *gugu*, the name of a bird; and (5) *kindi*, soft, as a woman's voice. In a second interpretation, social hierarchy is revealed; the master harpist, Delba, calls them: (1) married man; (2) bachelor; (3) married woman; (4) prostitute; and (5) young girl. An interesting comparison arises when these two interpretations are juxtaposed: something very strong is a married man, something of no value is a bachelor, one who gives justice is a married woman, a prostitute is like a bird, and a young girl is expected to have a soft voice. The middle string of the biggest harp, *galdama*, is considered to be the central tone around which all the others are tuned and played; the female association of its name, as married woman or one who gives justice, and its primary musical role reflect the fact that these exorcism rituals are for, and thus centred on, women.

Each part of the Fang Bwiti *ngombi* is regarded as a part of the Sister of God: her features are carved or sculpted at the top of the harp; the resonator is her stomach, her womb, the spiritual Source of Life; the neck and tuning pegs are her spine and ribs; the strings, her tendons and sinews.[26] Even the sound holes cut out of the sound table have meaning: the upper two are her breasts, the sources of her nurturance; and the lower sound hole is the birth hole. The music, the sound of the harp, is her voice, the female voice of pity and consolation, and with it comes special powers, mentioned above.

Musical instruments and cosmos

In some cases, the meaning of a musical instrument or ensemble so clearly connects the visual, aural, social and spiritual realms of culture that it manifests both the micro-cosmos and the macro-cosmos. The Bwiti *ngombi* has been explained as a single musical instrument which does so.[27] An entire gamelan with 24 instruments has also been shown to be, in its totality, a visual and aural manifestation of the Javanese triune cosmos and man's spiritual role within it.[28] Here, the symbolism of particular instruments in that gamelan will be explored, and their meaning postulated along a physical-metaphysical continuum.

The gamelan under discussion was manufactured (circa 1860) in Cirebon, the oldest court city in Java, on the border between Central and West Java (Sunda). In its culture, Cirebon is a syncretism of traditions and beliefs from both areas, with some additional Chinese influence. In 1893, the gamelan was brought to Chicago where both Central Javanese and Sundanese music were played on it in daily concerts during the World's

Figure 3: One of the two largest *sarons* in the 1893 gamelan: *saron demung*, female

Columbian Exposition; it has since been permanently housed there at the Field Museum of Natural History.

Just as the tuning of most bronze gamelan is individualised, so is the morphology (form) and decoration of their stands and resonators. All are carved or painted with designs that have cosmological or mythological symbolism. The most prominent and a unique feature of the Field Museum gamelan (known by its year of accession, 1893) is the morphology of the six *sarons*, bronze metallophones which play a kind of *cantus firmus*, the slow nuclear melody or melodic skeleton in a gamelan piece which all the other instruments simultaneously punctuate, or, embellish with faster moving variations and related melodies. The *sarons* are three-dimensional wood carvings in the shape of mythological tiger-lions, symmetrically depicted with heads at front and back (Fig. 3). They have solid coloured bodies like lions, but tiger-striped faces and manes. Like the rest of the gamelan's instruments, they are symbolically painted in three shades of ultramarine blue. Their teeth, fangs, eyes, manes, and paws are highlighted in pure gold leaf. On the sides of the tiger-lions, *nagas* (water serpents depicted with elaborate headdresses) are painted apple green, trimmed in scarlet. Seven bronze keys lie like ribs across each of their backs.[29]

Religion in Java has officially been that of Islam since approximately the sixteenth century. However, it is perhaps better described as a syncretic blend of Islam with beliefs from the original animism and the Hindu-Buddhism of the fifth to the fifteenth centuries.[30] The culture which resulted from the Hindu-Buddhist period in Java is usually referred to as 'Hindu-Javanese'. The gamelan tradition in Java remains primarily Hindu-Javanese evidenced in the decoration of gamelan instruments, the structure of most gamelan music, and the magical power invested in a gamelan.[31]

The symbolism of the tiger-lions is rooted in cosmological beliefs that are simultaneously dualistic and triadic. Dualism in Java, as in many cultures, is expressed in myriad oppositions such as night/day, good/evil, right/left and male/female; it is observable in the performing arts as symmetry, like that of instrument design and dance movements done first toward one direction and then repeated toward its opposite. Triadic relationships that are important here are the *Trimurti*, the Hindu Trinity of Brahma, Visnu and Shiva; the *Triloka*, the Hindu-Javanese triune cosmos; and humanity in the three stages of life: children, adults, and elders.

The cosmos itself is bipartite (two worlds) expressed conceptually as tripartite. In illuminating the *Triloka*, Senosastroamidjojo explains[32] that man develops his life between two world areas: the lower-world to which everything belongs that is related to his body and material outer-world (*Jana-Loka*); and the upper-world of gods and goddesses to which man strives with his mind and soul (*Ngendra-Loka*). His soul or mind (*Guru-Loka*) (the third part) is the link between the lower-world and the upper-world. And this is not only true for his own micro-cosmos, but also for the universe, the macro-cosmos surrounding him. Senosastroamidjojo adds that in order to penetrate into the upper-world, one must first be spiritually prepared, otherwise the mind could not bear the blinding light of the supernatural spirit.

The six tiger-lion *sarons* are in three pairs, each pair with its own octave range; the three pairs span three successive octaves. K. R. T. Wasitodiningrat, a highly esteemed, Javanese master musician from Yogyakarta, Central Java, informed me that the three members of each family of instruments in a gamelan are symbolic of the *Trimurti*, the Hindu Trinity. Other triadic symbolism is found in the three tiger-lions; they are sculptures of three different sizes representing children, adults, and elders. This is further evidenced in their teeth: the children tiger-lions have little milk teeth; the adults, strong teeth and fangs at the back of the mouth; the elders, no lower teeth nor fangs (Fig. 4). Sis Maryono Teguh, an East Javanese artist, explained to me that the lack of fangs symbolised the once common Javanese practice in which elders removed their eye teeth when they felt they were spiritually prepared and ready to give up earthly pursuits.

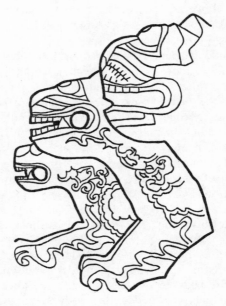

Figure 4: Detail of the heads in profile of the 1893 tiger-lions. Background left: *saron peking*, middle ground: *sarong barung*, foreground: *saron demung*

Figure 5: The six 1893 *sarons*, end views. From left to right in pairs: *saron pekin* (children), *saron barung* (adults), *saron demung* (elders). Females and males alternately from left to right.

Dualism in the tiger-lions is rooted in the fact that in each pair, one is male, the other female (Fig. 5). This is evidenced in their overall length and height and the size of their paws and teeth. It is confirmed in their paired tunings; the female octave of each pair is tuned slightly lower than the male, a practice still prevalent in Bali but now nearly extinct in Java.

Further powerful symbolism in the *sarons* is found in their basic lion-serpent motif, and the deeper, spiritual meaning of tigers. According to Bosch in Hindu art, the lion-serpent motif is symbolic of the creative, spiritual power operative in nature: the lion is the male element; the serpent, the female.[33] In Cirebon, the origin city of this gamelan, pairs of lions adorn the entrances of the palaces and are found as important motifs in *batik* design.

In Sundanese (West Javanese) belief, as in many parts of Indonesia and Malaysia, tigers have powerful associations. In Sunda, one may refer to one's ancestors, especially grandparents, as tigers. In addition, a famous legend surrounds Maharaja Prabu Siliwangi, the ruler of Pakuan Pajajaran, the last Sundanese Hindu-Buddhist kingdom. Siliwangi fought the Islamic forces who tried to take over his kingdom and convert it. Soemaatmadja explains that Siliwangi and his followers decided to become spirits (*Hyang*, *i.e.*, divinities); he adds:

'There are those who say that Prabu Siliwangi and his followers who did not want to accept Islam became tigers: *Maung Pajajaran* (Tiger of Sunda) say the Sundanese. This tiger comes each year, in the month of Maulud, to Pakuan Pajajaran's remains.'[34]

The tiger in Sunda is thus associated with both family ancestor spirits and with those of powerful demi-gods.

Pak Adjut Erawan, the caretaker of the sacred Sundanese gamelan at Lebakwangi, upon seeing colour photographs of the *sarons*, explained to me that they were unquestionably tigers and very powerful symbols. He added that the disguise of their 'tigerness' with solid colour lionesque bodies and legs, and the presence of manes (found on lions but not tigers), was a protective way of depicting the powerful physical and spiritual nature of tigers without danger.[35] The power of the tiger-lions was further emphasised by the manner in which gold leaf was applied to their teeth, fangs and paws: their weapons. Instead of being underlaid with red, which makes the guilding bright yellow gold as it is on all the rest of the gamelan, the teeth, fangs and paws are underlaid with light blue which makes them appear silver. This is reminiscent of the technique of using a different metal or jewel to highlight the destructive power of Shiva's third eye on statues of him.

The meaning of the tiger-lion *sarons*, with their simultaneous dualistic and triadic symbolism, can be postulated on a physical-metaphysical continuum. Beginning at the physical level with the tiger-lion *sarons* as material objects, the continuum moves through the physical, social, and conceptual levels of humans to the metaphysical levels of spiritually prepared ancestors and gods and, ultimately, to the cosmos as a whole. At the bottom of the continuum is the purely physical level of the lower-world with the three pairs of tiger-lion *sarons* as material objects, each pair with its own tuning (Table 1). Next on the continuum is the physical-conceptual level of the three pairs of tiger-lion sarons as symbols of humanity in the three stages of life: children, adults and elders. Following that is the physical-conceptual level of the tiger-lions as male and female in each pair, tuned respectively with male and female tunings. Next is the most important level, the musical-conceptual level of male and female children, adults, and elders functioning as a family, providing the nucleus (nuclear melody of melodic skeleton) of gamelan music and the nucleus of society. This is the level of the simultaneously dualistic and triadic interaction of male and female humans as a family in the three stages of life, the level in terms of which the entire continuum is defined. Next is the conceptual level of male and female, spiritually prepared ancestors penetrating the upper-world of the gods, followed by the purely metaphysical level of the *Trimurti*. Completing and ultimately capable of regenerating the continuum is the *Triloka*, the simultaneously dualistic and triadic cosmos.

METAPHYSICAL
- The *Triloka*, the cosmos
- The *Trimurti*: Brahma, Visnu, Shiva
- Male and female ancestors and gods
- Male and female, children-elders: nucleus of music and society
- Male and female in each pair, with male and female tuning
- Three pairs: children, adults, elders
- Three pairs of tiger-lions, each in its own octave

PHYSICAL

Table 1: Physical-metaphysical continuum: Symbolic meaning of the tiger-lion sarons

Summary and conclusions

The spiritual presence in musical instruments is evidenced by their essentiality to the efficacy of all manner of rituals and by the prescribed rituals and ritual procedures conducted to honour musical instruments in return. The spirits thought to be embodied in musical instruments, or working through them, are animistic spirits, or those of ancestors, gods, etc. The association of musical instruments with the spiritual world may be nearly universal; consider the western notion, expressed in iconography and elsewhere, that angels play harps.

Many kinds of power are invested in musical instruments and, in most cases, it is thought to emanate from their music, their very sound. Through their spiritual presence, musical instruments are believed to cure illness, instil physical strength, ensure successful farming and hunting, safeguard villages, and help with family problems, and facilitate spirit possession and exorcism. Musical instruments may serve as vehicles for communication between the worlds of the seen and the unseen. In some cases, their magical powers are thought to be accumulated by their owners. Power may even be invested in a musical instrument after it is no longer playable.

In their meaning, musical instruments incorporate the concepts that link the visual, aural, social, and spiritual realms of culture. These concepts may be expressed in aesthetic parallels between instrument design and other arts. The names for parts of instruments may simultaneously symbolise both social and musical hierarchies. Each part of an instrument may be considered to be a physical part of the spirit embodied within it; its music, the voice of that spirit. Or, an instrument, or even an entire ensemble may be manifestations of cosmological concepts. Thus, the meaning of musical instruments often lies along a physical-metaphysical continuum.

Through their voices and their bodies, their music and their material aspects, musical instruments serve as mediators between the human and spirit worlds. In the power and meaning ascribed to them, musical instruments have much to reveal about the religious imagination of mankind. One only needs to listen.

Notes

1. I am grateful to Donn Allen Carter, my husband of 20 years, who rendered the drawings of instruments in this paper.

2. Because royalty, including both chiefs and kings, are considered to be demigods or otherwise entrusted with vital religious functions in many parts of the world, royal instruments are often invested with spiritual power as well as having extraordinarily high social status.

3. For reasons of space, the examples for this paper, with few exceptions, are drawn only from African and Indonesian cultures. However, they have been carefully selected to be representative, as far as possible, of the spiritual nature of musical instruments worldwide.

4. For a theory of musical instruments and ritual with specific examples from

African, Asian and Pacific cultures, see S. C. DeVale, 'Musical Instruments and Ritual: A Systematic Approach', *Journal of the American Musical Instrument Society*, 14, (1988, in press).

5. The source for this paragraph is J. H. (Kwabena) Nketia, *Drumming in the Akan Communities of Ghana* (London 1963), pp. 6, 11–13, 16. The quote is from p. 16.

6. Drums, as well as various wind and string instruments, xylophones, rattles and others are capable of 'talking', especially in the many cultures of Africa with tonal languages. While instruments cannot exactly duplicate speech, certain textual features can be produced on them, such as syllabic tone, stress, and the intonation and rhythm of phrases and sentences. These are recognised by listeners, and instruments can thus be used to tell stories, send messages, invoke ancestors and gods, and praise sponsors and other members of an audience, even listing their genealogies.

7. The gongs in a gamelan range from 10 cm. to a meter in diameter; the metallophones, from one to three octaves. The tunings of the instruments of a gamelan span over six octaves, the same as a western orchestra. Normally, a gamelan orchestra has a tuning unique to it, based on a five or seven-tone scale. Consequently, all the instruments remain part of a single ensemble, known collectively as a gamelan. Thus, unlike a western orchestra where musicians own their own instruments, one person or community owns a gamelan and musicians come together to play on its instruments. Occasionally, gamelan sounding parts are made of iron instead of bronze; more rarely, of bamboo.

8. The traditions of correct posture and offerings for performances are usually respected by gamelan musicians around the world whether Javanese or not. There are now over 100 Javanese and Balinese gamelan in the United States alone. Most are at universities where they are used to introduced students to the music of other cultures as well as its meaning and function within them; they also serve as resources for contemporary composition.

9. The source for the information on the Newar is personal communication from Professor Ter Ellingson, to whom I am most grateful.

10. J. Fernandez, *Bwiti: An Ethnography of the Religious Imagination in Africa* (Princeton 1982), pp. 4, 365, 462, 464, 466.

11. In their design, variation in construction, and music, African harps are as unique as the 50 cultures south of the Sahara that play them; they are often sculpted or beautifully decorated. Nearly all are of extremely high social or religious importance; they are frequently the instruments of royal courts or provide the accompaniment for the recitation of oral history. African harps are small, normally with 5 to 21 strings, and are usually held in the lap when played. They preserve a great tradition: many continue to be nearly identical in construction to forms of harps depicted in ancient Sumerian and Egyptian iconography beginning about 2700 BC, harps that, quite possibly, originated in Africa in the first place. For more information, see S. C. DeVale, 'Harps, African', *The New Grove Dictionary of Music and Musicians* (London 1980), Vol. 8, pp. 213–216.

12. By now, the reader has probably noticed that this, and many other rituals for the spirits of musical instruments, is not unlike the common Catholic practice in which the faithful ask a saint or God to intercede for them, thank them for blessings, or otherwise honour them. In so doing, they place flowers or light candles at the altar of an icon or statue, or carry one in processions on certain holy days or their special feast days.

13. J. Kunst, *Music in Java*, 3rd. enlarged edition, edited by Ernst Heins, original edition, 1933 (The Hague 1973), p. 262, n. 2.

14. B. R. O'G. Anderson, 'The Idea of Power in Javanese Culture', in C. Holt, editor, *Culture and Politics in Indonesia* (Ithaca 1972), p. 12.

15. E. Heins, '*Goong Rèntèng: Aspects of Orchestral Music in a Sundanese Village*', PhD dissertation (University of Amsterdam 1977), p. 113.

16. H. Zemp, 'Ivory Coast', in S. Sadie, editor, *The New Grove Dictionary of Music and Musicians*, Vol. 9, p. 431.

17. H. Zemp, 'Music of the Dan', Bärenreiter Musicaphon BM30 L2301. Record sleeve notes.

18. P. F. Berliner, *The Soul of Mbira* (Berkeley 1978), pp. 186–190.

19. The sounding parts of lamellaphones are long, thin metal keys. The instrument is held in the hands and the keys are plucked using the thumbs and one or more fingers. The keys of the *mbira dzavazimu* are mounted on a soundboard and are therefore amplified for performance by being held inside the half-shell of a gourd up to 45 cm. in diameter while they are played. This instrument is uniquely African where it is widespread and has many different names, two common ones being *sansa* and *likembe*. 'Thumb piano' is a common English name.

20. P. F. Berliner, *op. cit.*, p. 190.

21. J. Fernandez, *op. cit.*, pp. 399, 416, 444–445.

22. R. Vetter, *Music for 'The Lap of the World:' Gamelan Performance. Performers and Repertoire in the Kraton Yogyakarta*, PhD dissertation (Madison University of Wisconsin 1986), pp. 32–36, 130–133.

23. *Gamelan sekati* are reserved for special ritual uses, primarily during *sekaten* week which gives its name to the gamelan type. They may also be played for the circumcisions and weddings of certain royal family members. This gamelan is believed to date from the mid to late eighteenth century.

24. H. Zemp, *Musique Dan: La musique dans la pensée et la vie sociale d'une société africaine* (Paris 1971), p. 234.

25 M. Brandily, 'Un exorcisme musical chez les Kotoko', in T. Nikiprowtezky, editor, *La Musique dans la vie* (Paris 1967), pp. 56–59.

26. J. Fernandez, *op. cit.*, pp. 365, 449, 538–539.

27. James Fernandez has elicited the remarkable symbolism and meaning of the *ngombi*. See, J. Fernandez, *Bwiti*, pp. 399, 416, 445, 449, 462, 466, 538–540. For an analysis of the *ngombi* in its ritual modes and an encapsulated view of it as cosmos, see DeVale, 'Musical Instruments and Ritual'.

28. S. C. DeVale, *A Sundanese Gamelan: A Gestalt Approach to Organology*, PhD dissertation (Northwestern University 1977), pp. 100–180. Ann Arbor: University Microfilms #7805248.

29. Gamelan music, like much Asian music, is layered and mono-melodic; *i.e.*, basically, all the instruments are simultaneously playing slightly or elaborately modified versions of the same melody. In Central Java, the melody that is played on the *sarons*, accompanied by the punctuation or marking of its phrases and subphrases by gongs, is the musical element that essentially remains the same between repetitions of a piece and between one performance of a piece and another. The variation and elaboration of the melody by other instruments, while subject to modal rules, are somewhat improvisatory in nature in that choices of melodic patterns or related melodies are allowed, as long as they coincide with the melody at predetermined structural points. Thus only the melody played on the *sarons* is notated for posterity or for teaching, and gamelan remains primarily an oral tradition.

The function of *sarons* in Sunda, which is not quite the same as in Central Java, but related, need not be explained here. Even though both Central Javanese and Sundanese music were originally played on this gamelan, and the gamelan was probably expressly made to do so, the musical function of the *sarons* and its meaning are expressed in Central Javanese terms. This is because the number and pairing of the *sarons* in this gamelan reflects Central Javanese tradition and not Sundanese where fewer *sarons* are used.

30. For further information, see C. Geertz, *Religion in Java* (Glencoe, Illinois 1960). For recent essays on various religions in Indonesia, see R. S. Kipp and S. Rodgers, editors, *Indonesian Religions in Transition* (Tuscon 1987).

31. See J. Becker, 'Hindu-Buddhist Time in Javanese Gamelan Music', in *The Study of Time* edited by J. T. Fraser, N. Lawrence and D. Park (New York 1981), pp. 161–172; and S. C. DeVale, *Cosmological Symbolism in Javanese Gamelan Morphology*, in press, Centre for South and Southeast Asian Studies, University of California-Berkeley. Dance traditions are also primarily Hindu Javanese as are the puppet traditions, the latter also have Islamic and Christian forms. Catholic wayang puppets are a magnificent example of the Javanese syncretism.

32. This is a summary of a translation [mine] of Dr A. Senosastroamidjojo, *Renungan Tentang Pertunjukan Wayang Kulit* (Jakarta 1964), pp. 203–223; for a more complete translation, see DeVale, 1977, pp. 139–140.

33. F. D. K. Bosch, *The Golden Germ* (The Hague 1960), pp. 50–61, 136–137.

34. R. S. Soemaatmadja, *Tanah Sunda: Gamah Ripah Wibawa Mukti* (Bandung 1960), pp. 97–99. I am grateful to Professor Kathy Foley for the translation of this passage.

35. As caretaker, Pak Erawan is entrusted not only with the physical and ritual care of this gamelan, but also with the oral tradition concerning the philosophy and meaning of the instruments and its repertoire. He is also responsible for ensuring that the musical tradition of each particular instrument is handed down in a continuous line from father to son.

J. H. Kwabena Nketia

Musical Interaction in Ritual Events

THE CLASS of events described in this paper as ritual events includes all organised activities that form an integral part of any occasion devoted to observances that follow a prescribed routine directed to some focus of worship or towards the achievement of some spiritual or religious end. The temporal boundaries of such occasions are usually marked by activities which begin and close the formal events. For example among the Ga of Ghana, a traditional ritual occasion always begins and ends with a prayer or a series of prayers (Nketia 1962). Each of the different phases of the occasion is similarly begun and closed with a prayer, thus setting off moments of separation of the secular or profane from the sacred, or moments of intense concentration on some corporate ritual activity from those moments when individuals may relax for a while.

The ritual process itself or the periods between rites may be filled with music-making or some other activity. Among the Dinka of Sudan, speeches made at a sacrifice are punctuated by choral singing, while prayers are accompanied or supported by acts of praise consisting primarily of songs or hymns (Lienhardt 1961, pp. 241, 244). The total duration of a ritual occasion may thus depend on the duration of the different rites, the intervals that separate them and the amount of time devoted to music-making.

The selection and use of music may depend to a large extent on the kind of rite and whether it is conceived as private or public, for there are customary rites (that is, rites that form part of normal behaviour), rites incorporated into celebrations and ceremonies, including confirmatory and status-marking ceremories, kinship ceremonies and commemorative festivals as well as rituals of worship.

Since the symbolic transformation that takes place in ritual is constituted by action which draws on sound, kinesic and visual codes, music which heightens the intensity of emotion generated by a rite or integrates the aural, the kinesic and the visual similarly enhances the ritual process. Accordingly, the music for a ritual occasion may include not only contemplative music such as charts and other music for listening, but also music that stimulates personal involvement in a ritual occasion through participation and interaction.

Interaction with the unseen

Musical interaction takes place in a ritual event when a group of performers engaged in music-making respond to one another or behave in a manner intended to respond to or influence the disposition, attitude or behaviour of a deity, an ancestor, a person or a group of persons. It is reciprocal and direct when musical action evokes palpable response but symbolic when response is presumed or mediated. Symbolic interaction is presumed when the lute player of the Konbomba of Ghana plays in seclusion to commune with this god, or when the Gabon ritual expert plays the *wombi* chordophone, the Yoruba devotee in Nigeria chants the *oriki* or praise names of his deity, or the Adangme ritual expert signs to find out from his deity what herbs to prescribe or what rituals to perform.

The scale and intensity of symbolic interaction generated by music may be influenced by how a people structure their world of unseen reality and their concept of worship. While many African societies recognise a Supreme Being or God believed to be the Creator of the universe, they also have a very strong belief in lesser spiritual beings and forces who owe their existence to Him (Forde 1954; Mbiti 1969). Because of the way these lesser beings are believed to relate to human beings in their daily lives, it is these rather than the Supreme Being Himself that generally serve as the main focus of worship and musical interaction in ritual events.

Some societies acknowledge the Supreme Being in their attitudes, prayers and songs, even though He is not the immediate focus of worship. Before an Akan priest (who is invariably attached to a lesser god) begins to dance on an important occasion of public worship, he points his dancing sword skywards to acknowledge Him as the power on whom he and his god depend. The chorus of women singers extol His name while the drummer of the talking drums reminds the assembly that He is the Creator of the universe and is from time immemorial.

The path has crossed the river,
The river has crossed the path.
Which is the elder?
We made the path and found the river.
The river is from long ago,
From the Creator of the universe.

In another poem the drummer reminds everyone of humankind's dependence on the Supreme Being:

The Heavens are wide, very very wide.
The Earth is wide, very very wide.
We have lifted it and taken it away
We have lifted it and brought it back.
From time immemorial,
The dependable God bids us all abide by his injunctions.
Then shall we get whatever we want,
Be it white or red.
It is God, Creator of the firmament.
Good morning to you God, good morning, Great One.

The Ga of Ghana similarly acknowledge the Supreme Being at the commencement of worship in the *kple* religious tradition. A chorus of men led by a cantor proclaims:

Man, lord of earth's life giving force
Looks up to God on high.
Earth sustains us, but God is supreme.
When the fowl drinks water,
It looks up and shows it to God on high.
God is supreme.

After acknowledging the Supreme Being in this manner, the singers proceed to address the lesser beings who are believed to respond to music that affects them and to participate actively in music and dance through their human mediums (Nketia 1959). Because of this belief, the concept of worship involves not just contemplation but also interaction, a mode of behaviour not generally considered appropriate when it comes to the Supreme Being, for unlike the lesser gods, He does not make himself manifest through human mediums. Nor does He need to be discovered, for knowledge of Him is given to all human beings at birth. 'No one shows God to the child', says the Akan proverb. 'If you wish to speak to him', says another proverb, 'speak to the wind', for he is everywhere. Thus the Supreme Being is a subject of philosophical thought, and speculation (see Danquah 1968).

In contrast, the lesser beings are often the subject of mythology, fantasy and creativity because of the extraordinary behaviour attributed to them, their capacity for good and evil, their frequent interaction with human beings, their heirachical structure, roles and functions, and the supernatural ways in which they reveal themselves. Acting through human mediums they are known to object to songs they do not like— those that do not communicate the message they would like to give or those that do not fill the dance their mediums have to perform at a given moment—and to ask for other songs to be sung for them. Because of this, some public ritual occasions take a dramatic form, with mediums appearing in masks or special costumes and acting in a manner that enables those present to recognise the spiritual beings they represent.

In some African societies, the practice of spirit mediumship extends to the ancestors when they are called upon for their intervention or assistance in times of misfortune or sickness, since it is believed that human beings are endowed with a spirit or soul which survives death and that they continue to take interest in the affairs of their living kinsmen. Among the Bemba of Zambia, the spirit of a dead royal musician may appoint his successor by possessing a living musician. Ritual experts are able to determine who the returning musician is by listening to the songs that the possessed person sings while undergoing therapy (Mapoma 1980). Similarly among the Shona of Zimbabwe, ritual events called *bira* devoted to the ancestors are held periodically. The principal instrument played on such occasions is the plucked idophone called *mbira dza vadzimu*.

Paul Berliner reports that

'In the context of the *bira*, the people believe the mbira to have the power to project its sound into the heavens, bridging the world of the living and the world of the spirits and thereby attracting the attention of the ancestors. In the hands of skillful musicians the mbira is able to draw spirits down to earth to possess mediums. At the *bira*, the members of the mbira ensemble are responsible for the possession of the spirit medium or mediums. Their music, moreover places other villages in a meditative state and inspires their tireless participation in the dancing, clapping, and singing which accompany the mbira music throughout the evening' (Berliner 1978, p. 190).

Another example of an instrument related to ancestral spirits is the *gingiru* harp lute of the Dogon of Mali used as a medium of communication with spirits by healer-diviners and which has several symbolic features.

> 'The focus of the symbolism is on the notched bridge: each of the sixteen notches represent an ancestor and a corresponding sentiment and character trait. The notches on the player's right represent social norms, and on the left religious norms. The power of the ancestors is invoked by placing the strings in the notches which are appropriate for a given ceremony. Their position is always symmetrical—two on each side, and resting in notches opposite each other. In this way the proper balance between the elements of the society is maintained and restored when necessary' (Knight 1968, pp. 17–18).

Since the lesser gods and spirits actively respond to music set aside for them, to perform music sacred to them is to invite their attention and active presence. When I got a team of *kple* singers of the Ga of Ghana to record the songs sung in the sacred grove (which I was not allowed to enter because I was not initiated), libation had to be poured as prayers were said and words of explanation given to the gods. They were not being asked to come down. The occasion was not an occasion of formal worship and the mediums who were present were to be spared the agony of possession trance.

Considerations such as these influence the choice of music for ritual occasions, for there are ritual occasions on which little or no music is performed. In some societies these include occasions for personal and private rituals, and sacerdotal observances that do not require the full participation of a ritual assembly. Further, the musical genres or items set aside for those ritual occasions concerned with the affirmation of structural relationships, celebrations of the life cycle, or rituals connected with the installation of chiefs and certain community activities may be differentiated in many respects from the sacred music of the gods.

Occasions of a mixed nature arise when a priest, a medium, or some person dedicated to a god dies, or where the worship of a state god is included in the routine of an annual harvest or commemorative festival. In such contexts, the sacred music of the gods and other kinds of music may be used, sometimes at different phases of the occasion. The funeral of a medium I watched in Accra, the capital of Ghana, had this mixed character, for it involved enactment of her religious status as well as her relations with the rest of the community. Accordingly, while performances of elaborate *kple* religious rituals and music dominated the programme, other types of music such as *adowa* performed by a chorus of women and *obonu*, the drum music of chiefs, were also performed.

In addition to mixed ritual occasions, there are occasions on which only music sacred to the focus of worship is performed: occasions set aside in the ritual calender for possession dances and religious festivals as well as special occasions of public ritual. There is evidence that in this context, music-making is in itself sometimes conceived as a rite, since it is believed that the focus of worship can be awakened or affected by it. The Mbuti Pygmies of the Ituri Forest of Zaire provide a good example of this mode of symbolic interaction. As Moke, an elderly man told Colin Turnbull, there are occasions on which the Mbuti sing to wake up the 'forest', for they know from experience that,

> Normally everything goes well in our world. But at night when when we are sleeping, sometimes things go wrong, because we are not awake to stop them from going wrong. Army ants invade the camp; leopards may come and steal a hunting dog or even a child. If we are awake, these things would not happen. So when something goes wrong, like illness or bad hunting or death, it must be because the forest is sleeping and not looking after his children. So what do we do? We wake it up. We wake it up by singing to it, and we do this because we want it to awaken happy. Then everything will be well and good again. So when our world is going well, then also we sing to the forest, because we want it to share our happiness.

As Moke further explained to Turnbull, the Mbuti do not know exactly what their deity of the forest is like.

> How can we know? We can't see him; perhaps when we die we will know
> and then we can't tell anyone. So how can we say what
> he is like or what his name is? But he must be good to give us
> so many things. He must be of the forest. So when we sing,
> we sing to the forest.

Commenting on 'the complete faith of the Pygmies in the goodness of their forest world', Turnbull observes that

> At no point do their songs ask for this or that to be done, for the hunt

to be made better or for someone's illness to be cured. It is not necessary. All that is needful is to awaken the forest, and everything will come right. But suppose it does not, suppose that someone dies, then what? Then the men sit around the evening fire, and they sing songs of devotion, songs of praise, to wake up the forest and rejoice it, to make it happy again. Of the disaster that has befallen them, they sing, in this one great song. There is darkness around us; but if darkness *is*, and the darkness is of the forest, then the darkness must be good' (Turnbull 1962, p. 93).

Interaction within the ritual assembly

The significance of the music of a ritual occasion does not lie only in the symbolic interaction it generates, but also it means it provides for the affirmation of communal values and the renewal of the bonds and sentiments that bind a community or the devotees of a god, for in traditional African societies, the repertoire of religious songs is not always devoted exclusively to the focus of worship. For example the repertoire of *kple* songs of the Ga of Ghana includes songs that refer to incidents to their social history, migrations and wars, songs about their neighbours, interpersonal relationships, as well as songs based on proverbs and other sayings. The singing of lampoons is incorporated into the La Kpa festival celebrated by one of the communities because it is believed to have been ordained by their god for the purpose of re-ordering social relations which invariably become strained during the year. Instead of such songs, in another Ga community the rules of the festival insist on the settlement of quarrels on the morning of the day of the great feast, while the possession dance, the climax of the festival, is performed later in the afternoon. All traditional Ga prayers include a formula for peace and unity.

A similar concern for order, for ethical and social values, is shown by communities in their Brong Ahafo region of Ghana who worship the god Ntoa, all of whom organise a special festival annually at which lampoons are sung. In Wenchi, one of the states in this area, the singing of such songs takes a very elaborate form and lasts for a whole week.

The inauguration of the festival starts with a ritual event in the precinct of the temple of the good attended priests, ritual officers, and elders of the town. This god is regarded as a god of fertility and rain and is addressed as *nana* (grandsire), *kunu* (husband), *se* or*agya* [*father*]. *His worshippers are referred to as his children* [*ne mma*) for he is a personal guardian, a god that protects his children from evil powers and witchcraft. He is a tower of help (*boaban*), chief helper (*oboa-hene*) and a safe prop (*tetantwere*) as the following song proclaims:

'When I lean against father,
It is like leaning against a rock:
   a safe prop.
Ntoa Kofi has taken me for a child to be protected.
Nana has offered to guard me.
I have nothing to fear in the bush.
Osei Kofi has taken me for a friend.'

When the details of the year's celebration have been determined, three ritual officers bring the shrine of the god out of the temple and place it in front of the door. The elders take their seats near it. Each one then takes an egg he has bought with him and offers it the god. (The eggs are broken as they are offered). After the egg offering, they all go back to their seats until they are called to pour libation to god. Again the officers retire. A sheep is sacrificed. One of the ritual officers goes to the temple and tells the god, 'We have finished', He strikes a special drum in the temple thrice. All those outside the temple join in a chant. As soon as it ends, the heavy drum ensemble outside the temple is played. Bells are sounded when the drums stop. The shrine of the god is carried away for a short distance accompanied by the bells and brought back This is done three times.

When all the sacrifices have been made, those in attendance proceed in a party, together with the shine, to a special ritual spot in a grove where further rites are performed and the shrine immersed in water to purify it. There is a short spell of music and ceremonial dancing. Seven of the elders take turns at performing this dance. After this the shrine of the god is brought back to the temple to the accompaniment of the sound of bells. As they get close to the temple, a gun is fired, and everyone is commanded to go away, leaving the ritual officers who return to the sanctuary. From this time until the whole festival is over, no one can be accused of any wrong or charged with any criminal offence. People are at liberty to say what they like in song—to insult, critise, challenge anyone, including those in authority and go scot free. The singing is usually done by organising groups who go from one end of the town to the other. The style of these songs which is accompanied by drums and rattles is different from the song repertoire sung for possession dances (Nketia 1964, pp. 144–205).

On the final day of the festival, a performance attended by the chief and elders of the town, the ritual officers, and all interested members of the town takes place in an open space near the temple of the god. Three singing groups reflecting the traditional political organisation of the town, *Asere Bokoro* and *Konton* take part. The *Asere* representing the royal clan and *Konton* representing the commoners contend, singing insulting songs about each other or songs of praise in defence of themselves or anyone of their number. They sing from opposite ends of the arena and move in a direction parallel to the temple. They brush past each other in the middle of the arena and are thus able to hear what the other party is singing. As soon as they get to the other end, they think of a suitable retort and sing it in the next song. The third group choses a different route from that of two contending parties for they are the peace makers.

The event is concluded with a show of strength by the young men of the two contending singing groups. At the command of an elder in charge of the ceremony, the two groups of young men lift a long pole placed between them and try to push the other away from its side of the pole. The festival is concluded by the priests and elders with further rites and drumming. It is expected to rain or shower on the final night, or soon afterwards.

Interacting and rejoicing with music and dancing in the context of ritual and worship is also an important aspect of the African concept of religious expression and may be given free reign at religious festivals. When Orisha Oko, normally worshipped in Yorubaland by women at the new moon, is worshipped by the whole community after the harvest, feasts in the home are 'followed by general merriment, including processions and dances' (Lucas 1984, p. 110).

Similarly the opening event of the *kpledzo* festival celebrated by the Ga people of Tema, a coastal town in Ghana, is conceived as a musical occasion for general rejoicing and merry making. It is an occasion for all sections of the community of worshippers to interact in musical performances—the uninitiated laity, the initiated laity, the *agba* or priestly group which includes the elders of the town; the *kple* musicians consisting of the principal cantor (*olai*) and the drummers, mediums of the gods and the priests of all the household gods of the community. Before the ritual assembly gathers at the public sanctuary, the inhabitants of the town are expected by custom to organise themselves into performing groups on the basis of kinship or the voluntary associations to which they belong, and make music around the town. Elderly men and women may form their own little group and sing songs of prayer for food and fecundity for the youth, or for peace and prosperity, while the other groups sing some of the songs of *kple* stamping dance, or any other songs they like to the accompaniment of idiophones such as finger bells or any suitable sound-producing objects such as cans, for throughout this festival no drums other than the drums of the gods may be played, and these are played only by the drummers in the priestly group. The performance of all music outside ritual contexts is also banned during the festival.

Each group moves from one end of the town to the other without regard to what other groups are doing. Some may skip, jump or somersault now and then, while others dance all the way. To enhance the gaiety and festive atmosphere of the occasion, some of the participants may come dressed as nurses or priests, while others impersonate beggars draped in sackcloth or fishing nets. Men may dress as women, while some women dress as men.

Many of the inhabitants of the town who live and work in other parts of Ghana also return on this occasion to participate actively in the festival. They arrive in many lorries (covered trucks) dressed in distinctive costumes, singing and making merry as they form groups according to the cities from which they have come. They sing standard songs from the *kple* repertoire or songs about their experiences outside their home town, while those among them who lost relatives whose funeral they could not attend sing spontaneous dirges now and then.

The bustle in the streets comes to a head at about four o'clock in the afternoon when the groups meet for a formal act of worship. The senior priest of the town and his group come in a procession to the open sanctuary and take their seats. This procession is led by the *kple* drummers, followed by a stool carrier, two men carrying pots of millet beer, a horn blower, the mediums of the gods and other members of the priestly group, and lastly the senior priest of the town. A special ritual drum called *nyaado* is played in the procession, while the horn blower plays in the background in praise of the senior god of the town.

After the members of the priestly band have taken their seats in the sanctuary, the senior priest walks backwards some ten to fifteen yards, pours libation as he prays and returns to his seat. A drink of millet beer is served first to the senior priest and then to other members of the priestly group. Dancing at the sanctuary begins immediately after this. All the groups come near the drummers and await their turn to perform. As soon as a group comes close to the priestly group, their leader starts to sing a song of his choice. The *kple* drummers play the appropriate accompanying piece while the chorus joins their leader and dance vigorously as they sang. After a while they are beckoned off. Another group takes their place, while the *kple* drummers again provide the necessary accompaniment. Scenes of dancing are presented in quick succession until each group gets its turn. Libation is poured while prayers are said to conclude the formal aspect of the event. After this any members of the priestly group who wish can retire while the drummers continue to play for the entire ritual assembly to sing and dance for as long as they wish.

Interaction in the music-making process

The interaction that takes place on ritual occasions is not confined to musical behaviour that seeks to establish a relationship with the unseen or affirm the bonds of a common faith and shared values that bind members of a ritual assembly. It extends to the music-making process itself in order to ensure not only effective communication but also the required atmosphere for action and interaction. Indeed the non-availability of those who play vital leadership roles in ensembles such as a master drummer or a cantor can ruin effective interaction since it is these that provide the cues for those who have to perform particular rites, sustain acts of prayers and sacrifice and heightened emotion, create and maintain the energy levels required by mediums, or lead a ritual assembly in the singing of songs.

It is because of this that among the Ga of Ghana cantors, drummers, horn-blowers and all others who contribute to musical interaction on ritual occasions are made a part of the priestly group (*agba*.) To ensure their availability on a regular basis, they are made to go through the initiation rite called *Kromosto* that raises the religious status of a person and qualifies him to enter all the sacred precincts of *kple* worship. This means that whenever music is needed, there will be specialists to assist in the ritual process. Because of this they are also expected to be familiar with the routine of the different rituals, and to have a good knowledge of the repertoire of songs, drumming and dancing and of course the technical skills required in performance so that they can interact with priests, mediums and the ritual assembly. On the same basis some knowledge of the music and dance of the religious group is expected of the other members of the priestly band since they may now and then assume brief leadership roles, join in the chorus or enter the dance arena particularly at the opening of a dance event, and in the case of mediums, also act as the central focus of performances of possession dances.

In general the scope for interaction within the music making process itself is not as great in music designed for formal presentation as music which provides for creative performance and spontaneous expression. It is the latter that follows for improvisation and the variations required by changing contexts, as well as the use of elements of play and interplay, dialogue, signalling cueing, interpolation and superimposition of layers of sound on on-going sound events and a variety of other forms of spontaneous expressions that reflect the intensity of the mood of performers. Accordingly, in such music the performance focus is not only on the 'parts' specified in the design of the music, but also on the musical roles or functions that each performer assigned a given part has to play.

There are for example, the roles of those who perform ostinato patterns throughout a piece, the bell player who rings or strikes it at critical moments in a ritual or plays it to provide a time reference for a chorus or an instrumental ensemble, the drummer who plays in the signal, speech and dance modes and who guides or controls subtle changes in the movement of dancers or in the performance of an ensemble, and singers who chant or recite sacred texts in appropriate contexts, and so on.

Every culture in which music has this flexibility invariably develops not only repertories of songs and instrumental pieces, but also performance codes and procedures of music-making some of which may be applied generally, while others are emphasised in particular contexts. For example the Ga of Ghana distinguish between the manner of singing the songs of *kple* from that of recreational songs even though both of them make use of 'call and response. Speech-like chanting and deliberate annunciation of song texts set singing apart in the second performance context. The *kple* chant is performed at specific moments of worship or ritual as a prayer and a shout of exhilaration. It may be recited at the beginning and close of a rite. For example at a sowing rite, it is chanted after each person taking part in the ceremony has completed his turn. At possession dances it is sung whenever a medium shows signs of getting possessed, or wherever there is the desire to induce a much-awaited possession trance. Some members of a ritual assembly chant it spontaneously whenever they wish to give vent to their emotions. As it is designed in the call and response form, every time someone begins it, as many of those present as are aroused spontaneously respond and sing it to the end.

Similarly when a cantor begins a *kple* song, he may sing it in a free recitative style, repeating the couplet on which it is based on two or three times, adding other words here and there but giving a clear indication of the lines that must be sung by the chorus when it joins in. As soon as he finishes his annunciation of the song, he starts to sing in strict time. This is the signal for the chorus to come in and sing their response, and also for the drummers who have been waiting to begin the dance piece that goes with the song. The melodic form of *kple* is also differentiated from other Ga melodies, for the chorus response is invariably based on just two tones a minor third apart, each of which may be sung to one verbal phrase or sentence regardless of the tones of the words. As the Ga language is a tone language, this stylistic disregard of the tones of the constituent words is a significant difference between *kple* and other Ga songs and tends to enhance its ritual value (see Nketia 1958). The style and routine of *kple* dances are similarly differentiated from other Ga dances. The establishment of such stylistic conventions is indeed a common practice in African societies, for the forms set apart in this manner are often held in high esteem and generally attract those who are not members of a religious group to public ritual events as spectators.

Conclusion

In this paper we have concentrated on the behavioural aspects of music performed on ritual occasions in order to demonstrate, through ethnographic examples chosen from a few societies in Africa, how people's approach to the nexus relationship between music and ritual is determined by their belief system, the forms of musical expression and communication they cultivate, the meanings they assign to specific sounds and movements and the modes of interaction they establish in ritual and worship. As we have seen music may precede, accompany or follow rites. It may sustain a ritual occasion or give contextual definition to rites. It may serve as a vehicle of worship and communication with the unseen as well as an avenue for strengthening the bonds that bind the members of a community or a ritual assembly. Accordingly, ritual occasions differ not only in the ends that are pursued, but also in the complexity of the forms of behaviour or movement patterns and symbols intergrated with the sounds of music, the physical and temporal settings in which music takes place as well as the scale and intensity of the musical interaction that takes place.

It is because of the varying forms of behaviour, the functions of music in ritual contexts, and the evidence that music can be attributed with ritual value that Radcliffe-Brown once suggested that 'an anthropological study' (or as we would now put it, an enthnomusicological study) 'of the relations between music (and dancing) would provide some interesting results' (1965, p. 158), for as Parrinder;s account of *Worship in the World's Religions* shows, various integrations of music and ritual are practised in different religions. There is thus an ethnographic or cultural perspective from which musical interaction in ritual events can be viewed, irrespective of whether such events occur in literate or pre-literate societies, in temples or open places, in homes or sanctuaries. Such a perspective enables one to approach the meaning and significance of musical interaction from the point of view of participants in ritual events. It is certainly important for understanding what music making in ritual contexts means to African peoples.

Bibliography

Berliner, Paul, *The Soul of Mbira* (Berkeley 1978).
Danquah, Joseph B. *The Akan Doctrine of God: A Fragment of Gold Coast Ethics and Religion* (London 1968).

Forde, Darryl (ed.) *African Worlds: Studies in the Cosmological Ideas and Social Values of African Peoples* [*London*].

Knight, Roderic, *An Analytical Study of the Music of the Kora: A West African Harp Lute*, M A Thesis, UCLA 1968.

Lienhardt, Godfrey, *Divinity and Experience* (Oxford 1961).

Lucas, J. Olumide, *The Religion of the Yoruba* (Lagos 1948).

Mapoma, Mwesa, *The Determinants of Style in the Music of Ngomba*. PhD Dissertation, UCLA 1980.

J Mbiti, John, *African Religion and Philisophy* (London 1969).

Nketia, J. H. Kwabena, 'Traditional Music of the Ga People', (1958) *Universitas* 4 (3), pp. 76–80, *African Music* 2 (1), pp. 21–27; 'African Gods and Music' (1959) *Universitas* 4 (4), pp. 3–7; 'Prayer at Kple Worship', (1962) *Ghana Bulletin of Theology* 2 (4), pp. 19–24: *Folk Songs of Ghana* (Accra 1974).

Parrinder, Geoffrey, *Worship in the World's Religions* (Totowa New Jersey 1959).

Radcliffe-Brown, A. R. *Structure and Function in Primitive Society* (New York 1965).

Turnbull, Colin, *The Forest People: A Study of the Pygmies of the Congo* (New York 1962).

PART IV

The Catholic Theological Tradition

Adrien Nocent

Word and Music in the Liturgy

HAS THE problem of the links between word and music in the celebration of worship always been raised so persistently as it is today? Did it cease to exist at some privileged moment which serves as a model? Are there still possible suggestions to be made which do not repeat what has so often been said already?

1. Word and music in the Jewish religion

In the primitive civilisations, the first songs of creation are considered as creating the light, and the effectiveness of worship is attributed to the sung word and the music. The creator is song, and man, born of the sound of the divine word, is himself resonant. By association, instruments are divine and the skin of sacrificed animals is used for percussion instruments. But there certainly do not exist religions like the Jewish religion in which the word is fundamentally understood as an action which slips into a sonority. It is a phenomenon of incarnation, the music being like an incarnation of divine thought which expresses itself in song. This then presents itself strictly as fullness of the word, realised in a sort of sacramentality. The Old Testament fails to avoid the particular sterility of a balance between content and container, between signifier and signified. Although many instruments are used (*e.g.* Gen. 4:21, 31:27; Ex. 15, 19, 20, 32:17–18; Numbers 10; Joshua 6:4–20; Judges 5, 7, 11:34, 21:21; 1 Sam. 10:5, 13:3, 16:16–23, 18:3; 2 Sam. 6, 19:35; Isaiah 5:12, 16:11, 23:15; Ezek. 26:13; Neh. 12:27–41; 1 Ch. 15:16–28, 16:5–7, 25:1–7; Ch. 5:11–13, 9:11, 29:25–27, 34:13; Dan. 3:3–

15, etc.) they are suspect. Isaiah anathematises the Kinnor, the Nebel, the Hallel and the Toph. These instruments are an obstacle to prayer (Isaiah 5:12, 16:11, 23:15). Ezekiel considers music as a symbol of luxury and the evil life; Tyrus is his target (Ezek. 26:13). For Job only the wicked play music, and he associates music with evil (Job 21:12, 30:31). These instruments put the word of God into the anthropology of those times. They caused problems and the reaction was brutally surgical: all instruments were excluded, except the Shofar. And yet a song remained inseparable from the word, and the liturgy of the synagogue was completely sung. Each book of Scripture would have its proper song: a passage of Isaiah would not be sung in the same way as a passage from Numbers. Later, the Hebrew Massoretes, introducing the vowel-points in the text, would note above and below the *teamin* (tones) or the *neginnots* (modulations). The word was therefore always considered as inseparable from song. But it was not possible to integrate instruments into worship.

2. How the question arises in Christianity

Was this disquiet felt in the New Testament? We know that St Paul recommends song, and in many passages the New Testament is witness to the singing of hymns. But with what music? Like the synagogue, without instruments? Elsewhere, under Nero (54–68) we note a reaction against a scholarly music, inaccessible to the people. A kind of domestic music was created, situated between specialised music and popular music. Did Christians choose this middle path?

However, it may be, at the beginning of the third century the balance between word and music seemed fairly seriously compromised. In the first chapter of his *Protreptique*, Clement of Alexandria introduces a new song, succeeding the pagan song. The heavenly Word is the true athlete crowned on the stage of the whole world. Clement sets the new music against the pagan music and the Phrygian modes, for example. The Word sings according to a new harmony, a musical mode which bears the name of God; he has submitted the dissonance of the elements to the discipline of musical harmony to make a symphony of the whole world. Like the Word, Christ is song, music, no true music ever existed before him. As for us, we were already music before any other music; for we were in Christ before time began. For Clement, man is the only true instrument. The Word, despising the lyre and the cithara, soulless instruments, has with the Holy Spirit fixed our world and the microcosm which is man, his body and his soul; he uses him as a polyphonic instrument to glorify God and sings in harmony with this human instrument. Here, Clement quotes a text of unknown origin. Speaking to man, the Word says: 'You are for me a cithara, a flute, a temple'. He continues: 'The Lord has sent his breath into a fine instrument that is man, and has made him in his own image. He is the wonderful harmonious instrument of divinity, tuned and holy, supra-terrestrial wisdom, heavenly Word'. Is this a radical position to take? Clement adopts a more moderate one: 'If you want to sing or chant you are not advised against taking a cithara or a lyre, as the just King of the Hebrews did to give thanks to God. But our worship is spiritual and so the instruments are secondary'.[1]

Was this situation, difficult in concrete terms, experienced only in Alexandria? Let us recall two similar situations in widely distant regions, although in frequent contact with each other: Milan and Hippo. St Ambrose, certainly the most musical of the Fathers, so well-known as a composer of hymns that St Benoit in his rule called the hymn the Ambrosian, introduced the eastern antiphonal chant into his church. He had unreserved praise for congregational singing[2] and considered the singing of the psalms as an effective way of teaching.[3] But Ambrose also is hard on instruments: 'We sing pious hymns and you take the cithara? We sing psalms and you take the psaltery and the drum'.[4]

At Hippo, the case of St Augustine is more complex. In his time the Christian chant was only specified by the text, and the idea of a music reserved for worship is foreign to Augustine. His 'musical anguish' is well known. In this regard, a passage from the *Confessions* is classic: 'When I happen to feel more affected by the song than by what is being sung, I confess my fault and I would prefer not to hear the singer'.[5] Yet the experience of hymns was positive for him, but he did not cease to see in singing a danger of sensual pleasure. Singing is not necessary for the spiritual; it is a concession from God to human weakness.[6] He points the contrast between the *musica luxuriantis* and the *musica sapientis*. But the *musica luxuriantis* can become *sapientis* if it is well used.[7] In many passages of his work Augustine shows his agreement with song, so long as it helps interiority. One of his adages is well known: '*Sicut aures corporis ad cor hominis, sic cor hominis ad aures Dei*'.[8]

It is impossible within the limits of an article like this to recall the vicissitudes of the centuries which followed, when the celebration of the mass was seen to become a pious concert where the text was covered by the music. This was confirmed more and more in history, to the point when the significance of the proclamation of the Word progressively disappeared. Theoretically, the restoration of plainsong gave the Word renewed importance, but that was without real effect from the moment that the Latin text was not understood. To read in a modern language the translation of the text into everyday language before singing it in plainsong, or to write the translation below the sung Latin text—these are merely poor makeshift measures, worse than the simultaneous translation of a lecture, which removes the attention which should be paid to the lecturer. Here it is a question in worship of the Lord Himself who speaks to us today and in a mode of the reality of His presence.[9]

We will leave on one side the concert mass, a serious aberration fortunately rare today and carrying its own condemnation.

3. The problem in our time

How should we regard today the problem the history of which we have hardly been able to summarise in order to consider its elements more fully?

The question of the significance of the word in the liturgy is progressively revived; of course, time will be needed for this reawakening to become more generalised. But we must take account of a good beginning. Some may find the following reflection strange: contemporary song is very mindful of the text, which it tries to enhance by music and rhythm. I believe that the importance given to the text in contemporary songs could have an influence over the composition of liturgical chants today. Looking closely, one must admit that many contemporary song writers seem to have created models out of respect for the word that their music succeeds in promoting and which carries the crowd along. One could not say that for many of these songs the music is an ofject in itself; one feels on the contrary, that it has been studied to carry the word, and it succeeds in galvanising an audience. Please excuse the rather grotesque comparison. Can one say as much for the music of the Franco-Roman liturgy in the framework of a prestigious 'ceremony', monastic and clerical, which has succeeded in turning the faithful into admiring and perfectly passive listeners, forgetting their priestly function?

Alas, it is still possible today to come across aesthetic celebrations of this type, which a somewhat too outspoken young man described as 'celebration of the death of God'. We must resist the temptation to find a favoured time in the past and seek a model there. This is the easy institutional attitude, which bogs us down in stability with its models which just have to be repeated. The paralysing nostalgia of a time when the words of a single text were sung to the same music. And what music? In the compromising situation of a past where the text alone specified music which was used everywhere else the temptation was great, in order to avoid confusion, to create 'sacred' music specifically for worship. This meant creating a certain aura of strangeness, deemed necessary, and we have in this connection recalled the concerns of the Fathers. Are they invalid for us today? I do not think so. It would be impossible purely and simply to use the style of contemporary song in the liturgy. Not only because of a certain inappropriateness, but because one cannot tack words onto a musical text which was composed to convey other words. The quality of a composition implies an unbreakable link between text and music. This, moreover, is the reason why singing plainsong and substituting another language for the Latin text appears as an act of vandalism and can only produce a result which is beneath mediocrity. The experience of the past, like the experience of today, seems to have shown that contemporary liturgical singing, while having a connection with contemporary song, must however, distance itself from it, and that in accordance with what the song is in liturgy—a bearer of divine words which cannot make do with a song composed for words which carry another message. It seems to me a waste of time to concern oneself with those who reject *a priori* the use of plainsong, even moderated, for certain pieces which are by their nature not for wide participation; this is rather an infantile reaction.

It appears clearly that we should turn towards the future and new research. Someone has rightly written: One cannot refuse to 'help the word of God to fashion men'. And can we deprive the Church of its prophetic quality, very uncomfortable no doubt, and not allow men to express in their own musical culture their close link with the word of God? It is a risk we run, admitting that an immediate and perfect success is scarcely possible, and that we will need time, maybe even another century, which is little compared with the six or seven centuries which it took to form and ... deform plainsong. Already we know of some good achievements; others will follow. But what line of construction and development should we assign to this important creation, if there is one?

4. Example of the Prayer of the Hours

Before beginning with a warning and a list of the dangers, is there not a task to be assigned to today's composers which plainsong did not fulfill and which lies in the fidelity of the music to the word?

It is especially the case with the Prayer of the Hours where our own age can intervene bringing new riches. In fact, each Hour has its own characteristic, marked by the choice of psalms and by the text of the hymn. In most cases, plainsong has not composed particular music for these different moments, and, particularly at the great festivals, the chants of the Lauds are also sung at Vespers and in the same tone; the tone of the hymns is often the same for these two Hours, it is also the same for Terce, Sext and Nones. There is no particular tonality for the Hours of Sunday. So there is here an inadequate provision of music for the different texts at the various Hours which thus lose part of their identity. The place of the hymn at the start of the service, its content and its music are all crucial for setting the appropriate tone for that Hour: it is a matter of indicating the True Light, the resurrection, the Sun of Righteousness, divine knowledge. For this is how the ecclesiastical writers understand it.[10] Also, tradition assigns to that Hour precise psalms which should be highlighted by distinctive music. Naturally the Lauds on Sunday, the weekly celebration of the Eucharist, should have their own music, clearly different from the rest of the week. Also appropriate would be music, perhaps in a hymnal style, for the canticles of these Hours. The same is needed for the evening prayer, the time of stopping work. The sacrificial aspect of this Hour of sunset is linked to the memory of the Passion. The evening service has a eucharistic flavour, and the repeat of Psalm 140 in numerous liturgies bears this out: it is a spiritual offering akin to that of Christ. Here, too, the ecclesiastical writers emphasise these many aspects.[11] Just as the music of morning prayer should be lively and stimulating, so the music of Vespers should be serious and meditative.

The three times of prayer during the day also have their requirements. They have their own symbolism which we cannot examine here.[12] It would be possible to evoke the memory of the moments of the Passion on Wednesdays and Fridays, and to celebrate the coming of the Holy Spirit on the other days. These two memories could be differently illustrated from a musical point of view. Whatever the case, these 'daylight offices' and Compline should be simple, as far as the hymns and the psalms are concerned. As for the Vigil, it should have very contemplative music which favours the hearing of the word. The responses to the word should be the object of special care given their specific role: dialogue between the word and the congregation. It goes without saying that the singing of the psalms will respect their proper composition.

It should be stated that contemporary musical composition can bring here a new richness, rarely if ever envisaged up to now, and this could be to the glory of our age.

5. The Mass

Close study of the different parts of the Mass, Proper and Ordinary, leads to the same practical conclusions. There is little space in this article for development.

Is it an aberration to sing the prayers, the eucharistic prayer? Would it result in the stifling of the word? We have already seen that the Jewish tradition distinguishes the books of Scripture by their singing. Is it impossible to find a chant which carries the word? In any case, the prayers, the eucharistic prayer, scriptural readings, should never be simply read, but proclaimed.

But present-day compositions present a danger: that of diversification. Although in a concert, we may willingly listen to different types of composition, in one act of worship this diversity is harmful. If each piece should have its own musical identity, the pieces must conform to the same style. Here lies the difficulty which plainsong perhaps avoided, creating a praying atmosphere which our modern services with their disparate music do not always manage to establish. This is why, without copying the melodies of plainsong, some continue to use their modes. In this perspective, research of the type carried out at the Benedictine Abbey of Maumont, in France, and at the Cistercian Abbey of Rougemont, in Canada must be taken into consideration. For it must be recognised that plainsong has that quality of diversity but within a single musical genre; but this does not mean that for this reason we should confine ourselves exclusively to this musical form.

Conclusion

I think that what has just been proposed, after the recalling of the experience of the past, lies at a high level of research; but it is at this price that contemporary music in the celebration of the liturgy can reach its true goal: to be the fulfilment of the Word. It can succeed, already some works are reaching their ideal. But the fact remains that patient work awaits the composers, who cannot do without a solid biblical and liturgical training.

Translated by Barrie Mackay

Notes

1. Clement of Alexandria, *Protreptique*, c. 1, passim. Die griechischen Schriftsteller (GCS), Vol. 1, pp. 3–10. Sources chrétiennes, Vol. 2, pp. 41–57.
2. Ambrose of Milan, *Exameron*, lib. 5, 12, 36; Corpus Scriptorum Ecclesiasticorum Latinorum (CSEL), Vol. 32, 1, p. 170.
3. Ambrose of Milan, *Explanatio in psalmos* lib. 1, 10; CSEL, Vol. 64, 9, p. 7.
4. Ambrose of Milan, *De Elia et ieiunio*, 15, 55; CSEL, Vol. 32, 2, p. 445.
5. Augustine of Hippo, *Confessiones*, lib. 10, 33; CSEL, Vol. 33, pp. 263–264.
6. Augustine of Hippo, *Confessiones*, lib. 10, 33, 50; CSEL, Vol. 33, p. 264.

7. Augustine of Hippo, *De doctrina christiana*, lib. 4, 55; CSEL, Vol. 80, p. 32.

8. Augustine of Hippo, *Ennarrationes in psalmos* 119, 9, Corpus Christianorum Latinorum (CCL), Vol. 11, p. 2142.

9. *Constitution sur la Liturgie, Sacrosanctum Concilium*, n. 7.

10. Cyprien, *De dominica oratione* 35, CSEL, Vol. 3,1, pp. 292–293. Clement of Alexandria, *Stromata* 7, 7; GCS, Vol. 17, pp. 32–33. Hippolytus of Rome, *La Tradition Apostolique* (Münster 1963), c. 41, p. 93.

11. Hippolytus of Rome, *Op. cit.*, c. 25, p. 65. Eusebius of Caesarea, *Commentary on Psalm 64*, Patrologie grecque, Vol. 23, col. 639. Hilary of Poitiers, *Commentary on Psalm 64*, Patrologie latine, Vol. 9, col. 420.

12. Clement of Alexandria, *Stromata* 7, 7; GCS, Vol. 17, pp. 32–33. Tertullian, *De ieiunio* 10, CCL, Vol. 2, p. 1267. Hippolytus of Rome, *Op. cit.*, c. 41, pp. 90–93.

Joseph Gelineau

The Path of Music

AT THE pinnacle of the songs of human and divine love, we hear the voice of the beloved in the Song of Songs: 'Come, my beloved, let us go forth into the field' (Songs 7:11). Now this song is only inspired because of another voice once heard: 'Rise up, my love, my fair one, and come away' (Songs 2:10).

A voice governed the awakening of the soul. The soul entered into loving dialogue. It lost itself in it. But it was in order to find itself truly in the Loved One. This appears to us to be the path of music for humanity captivated by the voice of the Other Being.

In daring to attempt a theological and pastoral reflection on the role of music in the relationship between man and God—and more especially within the framework of the Christian liturgy—it has seemed to us that the two illustrations of the Covenant and the Passover would give us the base reference which we needed. Hence the following plan within which our reflections will be set down:

(1) All desires and promises were already present in symphonic creation and the voice of man speaking, but they were veiled and ambiguous.

(2) The Word incarnate was the herald of a new song, but it had to lead the song of men to silence in order to break out into an Easter Alleluia.

(3) The Spirit has given to the Church the eucharistic hymn entrusting it with crossing and reconstituting the cosmos and man until the song of love finally reaches its fullness.

(4) What consequences follow, at the point in human and ecclesiastical history where we find ourselves, for man and the music of our liturgies, particularly in the western world?

1. The voice

'Music unifies, rituals differentiate' (Seu-ma Ts'ien).

The vast majority of cosmogonic stories originating from the most diverse cultures call upon acoustic images to explain the origin of things, of animals, of man.[1] Everything happens as if the most intimate relationship which exists between a human being and his creator-parent was first perceived by man as being a resonant one: noise, sound, voice, music.

The fundamental symbolic power of sound and the voice can be explained by the fact that the first external perceptions of the human embryo are acoustic in nature: surrounding noises, mother's voice. The strange divine power of the voice and music derives from the fact that this message from another person enters me by the sense of hearing and invades me completely without my awareness of its arrival and its source. Long before being a linguistic medium carrying a decodable message, it is a pre-logical communication, preceding the word as articulated language. Even when developed in cultured music, even when linked to words, the voice retains its mysterious power to echo our origins, to announce the arrival of another—friend or enemy—to offer infinite dreams to the will.

At this pre-linguistic stage, sound can equally well be the sound of thunder, evoking the voice of a higher power, the sound which can reveal to us the intimate nature of every object: stone, wood, skin, metal, etc., the sound of the human—or divine—voice which represents the person himself in his uniqueness and holiness, the sound of musical art, developed by every culture for its social or religious rituals, for its private prayer, its pleasure or its dreams. Music as art would not have such a wide range of connotations nor such a strong capacity to stimulate if it was not rooted in the totality of the cosmos and the human body, if it was not allied so closely to the mind and to the Spirit.

It would be easy to pick out from the Bible, through the many different cultures to which it bears witness, the very many acoustic aspects which symbolise the religious universe and affect the destiny of man. The inventory would be extensive. We will confine ourselves to highlighting some characteristics which will affect the path of music, pre-Christian as well as Christian.

(a) The sacrifice of sound

To the one whose voice has created or called us, terrified or thrilled us, filled us with light or with darkness, quenched our thirst or parched us (the beautiful sound must at the same time be 'luminous and liquid'), the response must be to make the sacred offering of sound. If he no longer speaks and is silent we should take the initiative to cry to him in order that he should reply, for silence is death.

At this radical level, sound—voice or music—constitutes a sacred link with the transcendent being. The religious significance of the sacrifice of sound is global, at once evocation and adoration, invocation and praise, from the syllable 'om' which contains within it all the acoustic powers, to the vocal expression of a kyrie or an alleluia.

The sacrifice of sound is at the root of all cults containing song and music. In the biblical revelation, it constitutes a force which carries us from blood sacrifices to the pure 'sacrifice of the lips', already present in the prophet Hosea (Hos. 14:2) and taken up again by the Epistle to the Hebrews (Heb. 13:15). It will culminate in the 'sacrifice of thanksgiving' (*sacrificium laudis*) from Psalm 50, vv. 14 and 23, to the Christian eucharist where it becomes the sacrament of spiritual sacrifice.

(b) *With ritual and word*

A simple horn call or a spontaneous shout can constitute a sacrifice of sound. Yet at the pre-ritual and pre-linguistic stage sound and voice risk being limited to a passing experience capable of any interpretation, or an unreal expression of a desire for union.

The appearance of ritual and articulated language brought to music and the voice a first 'setting apart' which would allow the exercise of forms and symbols. With its two notes (1st and 2nd harmonic) the shofar (the biblical 'horn') is far more than an occasional alarm signal. A whole series of coded soundings, as much in their rhythmic and melodic form as in their ceremonial usage, make a ritual of each sounding. One could say the same for the African balafon or the Far Eastern gong. It is remarkable that, in all cultured music, the naming of the degrees of the scale or of principal melodies is semantically similar to the vocabulary of the law and norms of behaviour.

When the word intervenes, the sound is integrated into many different semantic fields which alter its possible significance. The law is digested in the sung meditation; the object of the lament is designated; the praise names its intended recipient.

The sound and the voice are then absorbed in a collection of forms and sacraments. Music and ritual call each other and interweave with each other. In becoming ritualistic, music plays the game of forms fitting to the founding stories of every religious faith—that is to say, for Christians, the

Bible stories and the sacraments of the Church. Conversely, in becoming musical, ritual opens itself to the force of sound which runs from the beginning to the end of time.

(c) *At the risk of magic*

To grasp the internal music of every being is to be united with him. It is also to have power over him. To name the one called upon is to manipulate the power of his Name which he has given us by revealing to us the resonance of his essence. Each of these two operations can be carried out in obedience—which, etymologically, is an acoustic relationship: 'to listen below' and 'to reply'—in respect and in gratitude for the gift received.

But there is a strong and permanent temptation to use the power of sound to one's own benefit; to begin the genesis again by acoustic science; to submit to powers, good or bad, thanks to the melodies and tones which 'affect' them; to manipulate the 'carmen', which is both song and 'charm' at the same time; to venture the incantation which is musical enchantment and bewitchment; to practise the evocation of the dead, etc. Even degraded to the simple aesthetic level, as is common today, music remains a siren's song. . . .

(d) *In favour of dialogue*

The just interplay of ritual and word protects us from magic: the ritual which submits to the rules of what is or is not 'appropriate', and the word which demystifies by naming.

But the sound-voice-music mystery is another's mystery to be discovered, welcomed, recognised and loved. Then the voice becomes a profession of faith: 'When I cried unto thee, thou didst answer me', a confident call: 'Yes, thou wilt heal me, thou wilt let me live!', with the loving union in mind: 'In thy presence is fullness of joy' (Psalm 16:11).

2. The Word

'Sacrifice and offering thou didst not desire; mine ears hast thou opened' (Psalm 40:6).

'And Jesus cried with a loud voice, and gave up the ghost' (Mark 15:37).

(a) In becoming flesh, the creative Word by which everything was made followed the acoustic path of men. He heard the voice of his mother who bore him. He received a name which gave him place and identity among men. He learned the sounds of his mother tongue, the recitation of the law, and the hymns of Israel.

(b) But he was called to a more complete hearing. 'When he cometh into the world, Christ saith, according to the Psalm, sacrifice and offering thou wouldest not, but a body hast thou prepared me' (Hebrews 10:5). And according to the Hebrew text, the speaker says: 'Mine ears hast thou opened' (Psalm 40:6): you have enabled me to hear, like God himself, the cry of the poor and the wretched on earth; to hear 'to the deepest level of my being what is written of me in the Law': 'Thou art my son'.

(c) When he raised his voice, he would denounce lying words, cries of hatred, drivelling prayers. In the direct line of the prophets, he would repeat: 'It is love I want, not sacrifices'. He denounced ritualism without love, hypocritical observances. He knew the invective of Amos and borrowed it when he entered the Temple:

'Take thou away from me the noise of thy songs; for I will not hear the melody of thy viols.
But let judgement run down as waters, and righteousness as a mighty stream' (Amos 5:23).

(d) And yet he, the proclaimer of the kingdom, also prayed the psalms according to the rhythm and tones of the synagogue at Nazareth where he grew up. After the feast of the Passover, he sang with his disciples the psalms of the Hallel (Mark 14:26). He commanded us to pray continually, and gave us a model for prayer: '*Abbouna d'shemaya*' in binary balance and rhythmic assonance. He practised the sacrifice of sound, prayed with ritual recitation, sang words and tones, for he took everything from the ways of men, except the sin of pretence and magic.

(e) But the way of Christ was the way of the Saviour: 'He is brought as a lamb to the slaughter, and he openeth not his mouth' (Isaiah 53:7). The day came when the Creative Word and the Prophet of the Most High was to be reduced to silence. He was silent before Caiaphas, before Pilate, and at Golgotha where they mocked him.

'In silence the Word
Died for us' (Good Friday hymn *Litanie des Heures*).

On the cross, it was with a loud cry that he gave back the breath of life which he had received (John 19:30). Everything was accomplished in this sacrifice of sound. Now he was able to descend to the Kingdom of silence, where the dead cannot praise the Lord.

Here, all the acoustic forms of this world, murmurs, echoes, sirens, charms, enchantments, evocations, magic words and incantatory rhythms are confronted with the single sign given to men: the sign of Jonah. All music stops at the edge of the empty tomb, a mere resonating chamber, hollowed out for a voice to come. . . .

(*f*) Then the Easter alleluia breaks forth. Not a trumpet blast as at Sinai, nor a chorus of angels as at Christmas, but a voice which must be recognised by its 'tone', the new way in which a name is pronounced: 'Mary' (John 20:16). The response of faith: 'Rabbouni' instituted a new dialogue with the One who thereafter received the Name which is above all Names. Thus the announcement of the Good News is launched again by the first messenger of the resurrection of the Son become the first-fruits of the living and pure praise to the glory of God his Father.

(*g*) The death of the Word made flesh thenceforth detached it from any ethnic, cultural, linguistic or musical particularism. The 'rushing mighty' sound of Pentecost created an acoustic area without precedent where everyone could hear and sing in his language the wonderful works of God (Acts 2:12). A new wind bore a new song: the hymn of the Church.

3. The hymn

> 'Not unto us, O Lord, not unto us, but unto
> thy name give glory . . .
> The dead praise not the Lord, but we will
> bless the Lord from this time forth and
> for evermore' (Psalm 115).

From now on the Church knew who it was invoking and to whom its hymn was addressed. We might have imagined that Jesus' disciples, following their Master's example, would have kept their distance regarding any form of religion, pagan or Jewish, blood sacrifices or sacrifice of sound. In fact, a Christian author of the second century dared to write: 'We have neither temple nor altar, nor priests nor sacrifices . . .'. He might have added: 'nor music, nor songs, nor instruments'. That is moreover what the Fathers of the Church would partly do by challenging the musical instruments granted under the old Covenant to the weakness of a still carnal people, but surpassed in the new Covenant where man and the cosmos are the true instruments of the Spirit.

In fact, the Christian religion would gradually be formed as if it was summing up in symbols and sacraments of the universe, renewed in Christ, the whole acoustic world of man and the cosmos. But it did so, one might say, as the opposite of what we have thought we have observed in the history of religions.

(a) Everything begins with the kerygma: the cleansed word, the double-edged sword, which calls out in the name of Jesus and saves the believer. From this declaration springs early Christian hymnody which is first of all confession of Jesus Lord, just as it rings out in Philippians 2 or in many different hymns of the Revelation:

'Worthy is the Lamb that was slain to receive power and riches, and wisdom and strength, and honour and glory and blessing.'

(b) On this kerygmatic and acclamatory foundation arises, thanks to rhythm and song, an important ritual practice which represents a basic historical stratum in the inculturation of the Christian religion.

So gradually rhythmo-melodic recitations and psalmody reappear. These practices are at the same time sacrifice of sound, initiation into wisdom, ethical discipline and loving praise. Preaching hymnody—or lyric preaching—in the manner of Ephraem, uses on the one hand the 'number' (syllabic metre) and 'tones' (melodies) for a more penetrating transmission of the preached message and, on the other hand, a rhythmo-melodic refrain so that the listeners can participate actively in the dialogue of the Covenant. Responsorial psalmody, which became widespread in the fourth and fifth centuries, uses the same values. On the other hand, repetition of the litany was developed for 'sustained' and 'intense' common prayer.

(c) From the sixth to seventh centuries important literary and melodic developments took place. These involved especially, in the East, the creation of the troparia and, in the West, the creation of musical corpuses (Rome, France, Spain, etc.) Literary and musical art as such then became part of the liturgy. It was also the period when a sacred and divine aura appeared to surround the whole of Christian ritual. Deep strata of the archaeology of religious man came to the surface again.

(d) In the churches of the West, the door would open wider and wider to the conquests of musical art: the melisma of the cantors, first examples of polyphony, *ars nova*, classical polyphony, concerted music, etc. Closely behind, musical instruments of different sorts also returned.

In the history of Christian worship, it is probably music which has constituted the part of ritualistic forms most subject to change, because it has always been the most immediately affected by cultural changes.

Architecture and pictures, written words, social gestures of respect are all more stable than sounds which pass and which are only belatedly and incompletely fixed in writing. More than this, in the West it is the Church which has been the principal melting pot for musical innovation.

But this symbiosis between the Christian sacraments and the music of surrounding society has had formidable consequences for the liturgy. J. A. Jungman has spoken of the 'centrifugal force' of music in the history of the Roman liturgy. The musical act always tends to acquire for its profit other essential aspects of Christian worship, like its kerygmatic function (the biblical message is blurred) or its community expression (the musical ritual act depends on experts).

In order to remain the song of the Bride, the music of the Church must constantly guard against many temptations all the more fearsome in that they are rooted in the pre-logical depths of man. Old demons are always there to divert the musical act from its proper aim.

(i) The first temptation is to wish to acquire the superhuman power, cosmic or divine, of sound. Its grossest form is magical practice through the use of sounds supposedly endowed with the desired power. A more subtle form is esoteric gnosis: one who has been initiated in the knowledge of mysteries by musical science has power over them.

(ii) The second temptation lies in the delight which rhythms and harmonies can give to the senses, even as far as rapture and trance. Through incantatory rhythms or spell-binding melodies or seductive tones, sound 'ravishes' man's power of thought and action.

(iii) The third temptation is that of worldly prestige. The agents of ritual sound find there a means of social domination. Star-turn cantors, already reviled by Jerome, still exist. The ecstasy of the tonal discoveries made by the polyphonists of *ars nova* or by the inventors of new instrumental possibilities is found more than ever in certain research into musical language and electronic sound. Indeed, the sumptuous sacred music of the princely courts of the baroque era is not entirely unconnected with certain media shows of today within the liturgy itself!

4. The song of the Bride

'The Spirit and the Bride say: Come!
Even so, come Lord Jesus' (Rev. 22:17, 20).

Between Pentecost and the Second Coming, the Church gives the same worship to the same Lord. But it changes its voice, its tone and its music according to the men who are praying. What is it in our own day? Vatican II wished Christian worship to be enriched by the voices and songs of all the races, tongues, peoples and nations. What can we say of the path which lies behind and in front of us?

The situation is very different according to whether we are considering regions where the encounter between Christianity and local culture is an old or a recent phenomenon. And among cultures of old evangelisation we must distinguish between the Eastern churches which have preserved their traditions and the western countries which have known Christianity, Reformation and modernity. To speak with authority of the situation of liturgical music in the cultures of recent evangelisation one would have to belong to those cultures. As for the liturgies of the East, the question should also be treated from within. We will therefore confine ourselves to the western world and to the Roman Catholic liturgy in particular. But this course is instructive for all.

The liturgical reform resulting from the second Vatican Council was effected with the twin aim of cultural modernisation and biblical and ecclesiastical re-entrenchment. As far as music was concerned, that meant on the one hand an opening up to music which could encourage the participation of worshipping congregations, and on the other hand the revival of forms written in the tradition of Christian chant, like psalmody, acclamations, litanies, etc. To judge by the creative surge resulting from this reform in the different parts of the world, the results are already very positive.

However, every reform issuing from a central power carries the risk of not reaching the deepest level of people's souls, forgetting the archaeology of their cultures and by-passing their real expectations. It cannot be denied that this is partly what has happened, since—according to the uniformist conception of the liturgy—a conception of ritual which was too intellectual and functional was added to the inevitably interventionist character of this reform.

At the same time there began to appear in the western world, in reaction against the industrial and technological society, many different trends like the search for ethnic roots, a reassertion of the value of art and feeling, a renewal of religiosity manifesting itself in very many ways, from the charismatic revival to the success of sects and esotericism. We would have to expect these phenomena to have repercussions on the liturgy and especially on music.

Certain aspects of this vast question are examined in this issue. Since any synthesis is quite impossible, we will risk indicating a few aspects, positive first, then negative, which seem important to us today.

(1) *The voice* which prays and sings does not only express and communicate notions. It is constantly evolving, firstly by its timbre, its quality, its accents, its tones. Any voice which is raised speaks even before we have decoded what it says.

It seems that our present liturgies—taking account of important variants according to languages and sensibilities—often seriously overlook the role of the voice. Modern separation which sets on one side the spoken, non-musical voice, and on the other the singing, musical voice, has caused serious harm to rituals involving the word. There is no absolute division or contrast between spoken and sung, music and non-music. At a deeper level, there is a unity of the voice in a range of tones and within continuous scale of modes of utterance which covers a wide register of forms and postures.

A rediscovery of the sacrifice of sound would held to overcome this dichotomy. The reappearance in the Church of speaking/singing 'in tongues' is certainly not unconnected to the pre-linguistic functions of the human voice which we have mentioned above.

(2) *The recitation* of set patterns (prayers, psalms, parables, etc.) gives to the sacrifice of sound the structuring of a connection with the One to whom we pray and of whom we speak, thanks to the images and symbols conveyed by the words (especially the Names of God which are used). From this spring adoration, supplication, praise, everything which makes up the 'body' of a religious faith. All recitation implies a rhythm and a tone, a cadence and inflections, all basically musical elements.

There again, it is a serious impoverishment of the ritual acoustic world to include in 'music' only song governed by the 'note' (pitch) and always to give pride of place to the hymn, neglecting acclamation, public reading, recitation of psalms, the Lord's Prayer (which, in the mass, is not a song but a prayer) and so many other acts involving words, from the initial greeting to the narration of the institution of the Eucharist (always chanted in the Eastern Churches).

We should add that in a turning point in society like ours, characterised by a breakdown in the transmission of culture and a general loss of memory, the 'recitation' of the great basic symbolic texts remains the fundamental means of any transmission of culture. Religious faith cannot do without it.

(3) *The modulation* of spoken words in Christian worship has its most specific expression in sung prayer. The two main areas which attest this are the Eastern troparia and Gregorian chant. Here we do not have music over the words or words under the music, but a melodious expansion of the word relished and expressed in faithful and loving prayer. That particular chant can only be born of texts which are frequently re-spoken and

meditated on at length. It is never separated from them to play a purely musical role. The revival of this sweet melodic-verbalism is conditioned by the practice of recitation. Otherwise it will be presented as having an impoverished musical role, whereas it is a prayer which deepens and flourishes.

(4) *The ritualisation* of the musical act is necessary to liturgical music. This accepts or takes on the 'rules of the game' which emerge from Christian ritual. So, through the course of history were created: the division of psalter into 'antiphons' of three psalms; the *octoechos*, or 'eight tone' system which did not originate from a musical theory of the modes but from an eight-weekly organisation of the calendar; the Gregorian antiphonary as a closed corpus of text with developing music; and when the Gregorian melodic corpus in turn became fixed, the *cantus firmus* required for the new polyphonies of the mass; right down to the 'mass' as musical form.

Current practice, almost entirely in the open, will have to find ritual markers in order to survive, and thanks to this necessity for formalisation, a possibility exists for inventing 'forms' which last and which allow many different uses.

Compared with these main paths, lengthily explored by human religious and Christian tradition, it seems to us that several present trends remain problematic.

(*a*) starting from the just principle that music in the liturgy should be 'common', accessible to all and practicable for the greatest number, we suppose that the media today offer us this common music and from it we draw our current models for liturgical music.

The availability and suitability of this material remains to be measured. Its availability: is it separable from the ethos which conveys it? Its suitability: can it give to the words and the rituals of the Christian revelation the chance of a satisfactory way forward?

(*b*) Another principle: the music of the Church must be fully ours, therefore contemporary—the only 'contemporary' music indicated here being that which the enlightened practitioners judge to be so. Today we can only have liturgical music worthy of esteem if the Church finally opens itself up to this music.

If we restrict contemporary music merely to cultured Western music post-Schoenberg, which deliberately distances itself from the common musical language of our contemporaries, then we enclose the liturgy within an esotericism reserved for a very small cultural elite. The usual response to that is that the music for the elite today will be the popular music of tomorrow. But nothing could be less sure in the present circumstances.

On the other hand, contemporary music can be a privileged area for spiritual experience and can open new paths towards God even for people who have no taste for the present liturgy.

(c) Let us now consider what is less a principle than a fairly general practice. It could be called 'false riches'. We might describe it like this: in order that our liturgies do not appear culturally under-developed and fallen from the great tradition of western sacred music (whose works we no longer have the chance of performing) we dress up quite simple melodies in sumptuous polyphonies and enticing instrumental accompaniments. Fairly typical of this are the sort of faux-bourdons and tonal homophonies, simple and rewarding, such as those belatedly adopted in certain eastern liturgies.

This path of compromise satisfies neither those whose prayer is hindered by such an acoustic display nor those for whom such music is without quality.

(d) Let us finally mention, in the cultural explosion of our time, the generally eclectic state of our programmes of liturgical music. It is said that we must cater for all tastes: the young and the old, the classic and the modern, etc.

But can we hope to reconstruct liturgical music in the absence of a ritual plan and rules?

A contemporary composer was recently interviewed on the occasion of the creation of a 'mass' for large orchestra and chorus to a Latin text, a work destined for the concert hall but bearing witness to the spiritual values of a believing musician.[2] At the end of the interview, this composer was asked what he thought of present day liturgical music. He replied to the effect that: 'In order to find a new breath of life, it should return to monody'.

This reply has a symbolic value. We dream of a certain abstinence which would allow us to recapture the taste for beautiful sustained sound, for the well-spoken and savoured word, the balance of modulation, length and timbre so rich for the soul in the symbolic allusions, like a 'sacramental' sound.

Just as a small piece of bread suffices for the Communion feast because 'it agrees to every taste' (Wisdom 16:20), so, for the sacrifice of praise in the Spirit 'which containeth all things and hath knowledge of the voice' (Wisdom 1:7), we desire enough beautiful music to awaken and nourish our faith, to carry it on the wings of melody and rhythm towards Him who 'must be pleased with all praise', but without hindering it with sensual pleasure, or standardising it in mass packaging, or inflating it with worldly prestige or stifling it under an excess of ceremony.

Would that not be the '*castitas*' which was for Augustine the characteristic note of Christian worship, composed of few signs, clear and accessible to all? Restraint and attraction, integrity and clearness, pure acoustic space for the duet of the Song of Songs.

Translated by Barrie Mackay

Notes

1. 'Every time in the myths of the creation when the origin of the world is described with the required precision, an acoustic element is introduced at the decisive moment of the action', A. Schaeffner, in *Histoire de la Musique*, Encyclopedie de la Pleiade (Paris 1960), p. 132.

2. We have not been able to include in this reflection everything which could be said about 'spiritual' music, either as a means of evangelisation or as an area of religious uplift. These aspects are considered in other contributions to this issue. They merit a thorough study which was neither within my intention nor my competence.

Editorial Conclusions

MARTIN LUTHER is quoted as having said: 'A person who gives this some thought and yet does not regard music as a marvellous gift of God, must be a clodhopper indeed, and does not deserve to be called a human being, but should be permitted to hear nothing but the braying of asses and the grunting of hogs'. The thought is roughly stated but essentially repeats Augustine's affirmation that to sing is to pray twice.

The major difficulty in editing a volume on music and liturgy has been to get the issue in focus. In the Catholic Church's liturgy people were deprived of intelligible words for many centuries so that their worship was dominated by sound and sight. Naturally Catholics are now anxious to make sure that the word is given its proper place and that it be not again drowned out by unintelligible sounds or by music. Unfortunately in hymn singing there seems to have been an illusion that the words have to be easy ones if the people are to participate. A comment made ten years ago might still be true in many a place: 'Music built around three chords, poor theology, and weak spirituality is still heading the lists'.

In the reflections on the western tradition of music in liturgy found in this volume one notes a dominant concern that the music be made to serve the Word. Feelings clearly run high between proponents of different kinds of music and we are not done with the discussion whether it is the need for good music which is primary or the need for a music which serves broad participation and the transmission of a text. We asked ethnomusicologists to contribute to this volume because we thought that some of the questions about the use of music, in older churches and especially in non-European churches, could be served by another sort of look at the place music has in shaping life and opening it to the experience of God. Ethnomusicological considerations are often of a kind that do not consider music primarily as something which serves words. They show that it is possible to address the issue of words and music from another angle. Music is a way of inhabiting the body and of situating a self or a people in time and space. It involves not only the sound of the human voice but the sound of instruments as well, and not only sound but body rhythms. One of the articles in this volume showed how an Islamic people marks off all time by sound and lets this sound measure out life in terms of service of Allah. Articles about the experience of black people, whether in Africa or in the United States, indicate the importance of body rhythm as integral to music and point to the music of voice and instrument as a medium of participation and communication prior to any formulated word. In this kind of tradition one does not simply write music to facilitate word. The use of word has to be able to pick up on what is expressed in music. It could be that much of the popular music of the western world not finding its way into church assemblies has its roots in this perception.

In the United States at present there is much discussion about the lyrics which accompany the music popular among youth and even children. These lyrics can be atrociously violent and sexy but one school of thought dismisses this as unimportant on the plea that nobody attends to the words anyway. Another school of thought claims that because this type of music seems to express a depth of feeling about life the words that accompany it serve to give some kind of formulated response to the feeling expressed in the music. The debate reminds us that it is important to attend to what music of its own accord communicates about being and living. More of this kind of consideration has to be brought to the use of music in worship. Indeed those responsible for church music, in whatever way, can hardly provide what is culturally suitable if they are unable or unwilling to plumb the depths of life — feeling expressed in popular music, both traditional and current.

Whatever the approach to music it goes hand in hand with an approach to God's Word. A classical approach to the scriptures takes these without more ado to be the bearers of revelation and is simply intent on transmitting them and their message to a liturgical congregation. A less classical approach is more attuned to the resonance of scriptural proclamation in a congregation, because it is more conscious of the cultural element in the scriptures themselves and in the selection of liturgical pericopes. It allows that the appropriation of the Word in worship is dialogical not magisterial. One Sunday in August of 1988 the day's assembly was offered the text from Ephesians 5, opening with the admonition to wives to be submissive to their husbands. The woman lector in the congregation where I was celebrating told me that she could not read this text. When I asked her why, she replied that it was wrong to continue to proclaim as truth what was easily discernible as culturally conditioned and in the long run discriminatory. The problem had more to do with how this scripture was being handled in liturgy than with actually reading and reflecting upon the text. The lector herself showed that she knew well how to read and interpret this passage. The words of the text were not to be confused with God's Word among us, but how could this be made clear in a ritual form in which every chosen iota of the Bible is solemnly tendered as *Verbum Domini*.

A certain use of music only serves to underscore this sense of scriptural proclamation and to impose the face value of words on a congregation. When the use of the psalter in the liturgy was revised a couple of decades ago, the reform eliminated any expressions of hatred, with rather exquisite attention to the suppression of the final part of Psalm 137. It was thought that a Christian congregation could not be asked to make such words its own, either in recitation or in song. Nobody seemed to reflect on the need to be in touch with a human cry of desperation in order to sing of God's mercy. If we have no place for the expression of the former where does God's mercy enter into human life? With an enhanced awareness of the commerce with God of people in Old and New Testament times, of the wrestling to let God be and of the manipulation of the means of God's presence, and of how much ideology shows up in the written canon, we cannot abide with an untroubled reading of the scriptures in worship. Music cannot simply serve the transmission but has to serve the question.

Music in fact serves as commentary on the text and in this sense aids its transmission. We might be inclined to think that commentary on words has to be made in other words, though we ought to be accustomed to the experience that voice inflection in reading is a mode of interpreting. This is all the more true of music, whether vocal or instrumental. There is a kind of sonal commentary which does not issue from expressed ideas but which is prior to them. It is a response on the level of feeling which may indeed ask for verbal clarification and orientation, the function of the verbal however being to gather it in, not to hide it. The sound needs to be heard before the word is given form. The cognitive response to the yearning of human life, to its alienation and to its urge for God is seeded in the affective of which sound and music are important forms.

Some of the articles, for example those of Stone, Hoffman, Jeffery and Kock, speak of the reluctance experienced in allowing the use of certain types of music, or indeed in some instances of any music, in formal worship. Music can be allotted totally to the secular or allowed on the fringe of liturgy, as with the folk tunes sung at the passover seder or the devotional hymns of catholic piety that serve paraliturgies. Ethnic groups with a strong cultural musical tradition, or people fascinated by today's popular music, seem to make a profound distinction between the secular and the profane, or between liturgy and piety, where music is concerned. Is this because, in Catholic terms, it is deemed to be among the cultural traditions 'alien to the gospel', or, in more universal terms, it seems contrary to the reverence that has to be brought to the things of God? Since music is one of the primary modes of measuring or inhabiting time and space, this attitude is very close to other feelings about sacred space and sacred time. Perhaps it has to undergo some of the demythologization to which these have been subjected.

In short, we appear to be at a juncture where the question of the right use of music in formal worship is only just taking shape, whether in young churches or in older ones. Every church needs a cultural appreciation of what is expressed in its own people's musical traditions or in the more contemporary popular forms. Even more deeply we all need to be more attuned to what it is in human life and in human aspiration that needs musical expression so that without it the seed of God's Word cannot be sown. On the one hand the task is made more complex because of a more critical approach to the scriptures and their proclamation. On the other hand it may be providential that a revived interest in the use of a broader musical tradition in worship can help communities to express the more complex forms of response required by a reading which, although it is critical, nevertheless does not lose faith in God and in the memory of Jesus Christ.

David N. Power

Contributors

MELLONEE BURNIM is an Associate Professor in the department of Afro-American Studies at Indiana University-Bloomington. She is an ethnomusicologist with a special research interest in Afro-American religious music. She founded Indiana University's Afro-American Choral Ensemble, and directed it for seven years. This group is a mixed ensemble of student singers, narrators, instrumentalists and technicians who perform music by and about Blacks. She has published articles in *Ethnomusicology*, *Music Educators' Journal*, *Black Music Research Journal*, and *The Western Journal of Black Studies*; and book chapters in *Expressively Black* and *More Than Dancing*. She has been a research associate with Brown University, Providence, Rhode Island; a consultant for the Smithsonian Institution; and a consultant for the Interdenominational Theological Centre, Atlanta, Georgia. She is a member of the Society for the Study of Black Religion.

JAMES CONE received his BA from Philander Smith College in Little Rock, Arkansas, his BD from Garrett Theological Seminary, and his MA and PhD from Northwestern University in Evanston, Illinois. His books include: *Black Theology and Black Power* (1969); *A Black Theology of Liberation* (1970); *The Spirituals and the Blues: An Interpretation* (1972); *God of the Oppressed* (1975); *Black Theology: A Documentary History, 1966–1979* (edited with Gayraud S. Wilmore), (1979); *My Soul Looks Back* (1982); *For My People* (1984); *Speaking the Truth* (1986). At present he is Briggs Distinguished Professor of Systematic Theology at Union Theological Seminary in New York.

DAVID DARGIE was born in 1938, in East London, South Africa and ordained priest in 1964 for the Diocese of Port Elizabeth. He worked in Xhosa and English-language parishes, and from 1974–78 was chaplain at Rhodes University, Grahamstown. He completed his BMus by correspondence in 1973; taught theory of Music at Rhodes University 1977–78; and began running composition workshops for African church music in 1977. Since 1979 he has been running the church music department for the Lumko Missiological Institute, now in Germiston, South Africa. In 1986 he completed his PhD on *Techniques of Xhosa Music* for Rhodes University, Grahamstown. His publications include *Xhosa Music* (Cape Town 1988); articles in various publications on Xhosa music, African church music and related topics; music handbooks and collections of church music through the Lumko Institute; plus the Lumko tape series of African church and traditional music.

SUE CAROLE DEVALE is Assistant Professor of Ethnomusicology and Chairman of the Systematic Musicology Programme at the University of California, Los Angeles. She served as Vice-President of the Society for Ethnomusicology (1985–87) and Visiting Curator for Ethnomusicology at Field Museum of Natural History (1976–80). Her speciality is the study of musical instruments (organology) which she views as essential windows to the understanding of humankind. She has published on harps around the world, especially those of Africa, on Javanese and Sundanese gamelan, and on the field of organology in general. In this paper, and in 'Musical Instruments and Ritual: A Systematic Approach', cited in this paper, she begins an exploration of the meaning and function of music instruments cross-culturally. In addition to her scholarly interest in music, she has been a professional harpist for 25 years and leads the Javanese gamelan ensemble at UCLA. She dedicates this paper to Sister Mary Ignatius, a Sinsinawa Dominican, who led her through four years of high school Latin and has since continued to be an inspiration and friend.

JOSEPH GELINEAU a Jesuit, born in 1920, is currently priest in charge of five country parishes in the Paris region. For 30 years he has worked for liturgical renewal as a composer, teacher (at the Paris Catholic Institute), writer (articles and books), contributor to the Roman *Consilium* and to the National Centre of French Liturgical Pastoral for the work of post-conciliar reform. He is co-founder of *Universa Laus* (an international research group for song and music in the liturgy).

LAWRENCE A. HOFFMAN was ordained Rabbi in 1969, and received his doctorate in Liturgy in 1973. He is Professor of Liturgy at the Hebrew

Union College—Jewish Institute of Relgion, New York. Active in the liturgical renewal of the American Reform Movement, he has chaired its Liturgy Committee, and composed *Gates of Understanding* a two-volume worshipper's commentary on that movement's new Liturgy, as well as the historical introduction to its current Passover Haggadah. Among his other publications are: *The Canonization of the Synagogue Service* (Notre Dame, Indiana 1979); *The Land of Israel: Jewish Perspectives* (edited: Notre Dame, Indiana 1986); *Beyond the Text: a Holistic Approach to Liturgy* (Bloomington, Indiana 1987); and *The Art of Public Prayer: not for Clergy Only* (Washington 1988).

PETER JEFFERY taught music history at the Universities of Delaware, Harvard, and Princeton, and was a cataloguer of medieval manuscripts at the Hill Monastic Manuscript Library. He is the editor of *Liturgical Chant Newsletter*, and has published in *Archiv für Liturgiewissenschaft*, *Ephemerides Liturgicae*, *Worship*, *Patristics*, *Judaica*, *Jewish Quarterly Review*, *Scriptorium*, *Speculum*, and *Journal of Musicology*. He received the Alfred Einstein Award of the American Musicological Society (1985), and he was the first musicologist to be awarded a John D. and Catherine T. MacArthur Fellowship (1987). His forthcoming books include *Oral and Written Transmission in Ethiopian Christian Chant* (with Dr Kay Shelemay) and *The Chant Tradition of Early Christian Jerusalem, and Its Role in the Formation of the Eastern and Western Chant Repertories*. He is an Oblate of St. John's Benedictine Abbey, Collegeville, USA.

GERARD KOCK was born in Rotterdam on 30 December 1935. He studied for the priesthood with the Marist Fathers. From 1961 to 1976 he worked as a community pastoral worker in Bergen op Zoom and 's Hertogenbosch. From 1976 to 1986 he was responsible for liturgical formation in the Oss deanery. In the later 1970s he was also studying at the Catholic University of Tilburg, where he gained his doctorate in theology with a dissertation on developments in church music since Vatican II. At present he is involved in giving courses to voluntary pastoral workers and writing material for groups with specific aims. He is a member of the executive of the Dutch St Gregory association and is on the editorial board of *Continuo*, the periodical for liturgy and liturgical music published by Gooi en sticht, Hilversum.

ELLEN KOSKOFF is an Associate Professor of Musicology at the Eastman School of Music in Rochester, New York, where she teaches courses in ethnomusicology. She is also currently a Visiting Professor in the Fine Arts Department at Syracuse University, and has been a Visiting Professor at the University of California at Los Angeles and, most recently, at New York University. She is the editor of *Women and Music in Cross-Cultural Perspective*, and has published in such journals as, *Selected Reports in Ethnomusicology*, *World of Music* and *Ethnomusicology*, where she also acted as Book Review Editor from 1982–85. Her research interests include music in urban contexts, music and cognition, and music and gender.

J. H. KWABENA NKETIA, former director of the Institute of African Studies at the University of Ghana, and Professor Emeritus of the University of California at Los Angeles, is Andrew Mellon Professor of Music and the Chairman of the Music Department at the University of Pittsburgh.

ADRIEN NOCENT is a Benedictine monk at the Abbey of Maredsous (Belgium). He was born in 1913, and specialised at the Liturgical Institute in Paris and at the Sorbonne. For 10 years, he was teacher at the Lumen Vitae (Brussels) and in charge of lectures at Louvain University until 1967. Co-founder and teacher at St Anselm Pontifical Liturgical Institute in Rome since 1961, he is scientific director of the magazine *Ecclesia Orans*. Author of: *Célébrer Jésus Christ* (Année liturgique) 7 vols. (Paris 1975–77); *L'avenir de la Liturgie* (Paris 1961); numerous magazine articles.

RUTH M. STONE is an Associate Professor of Folklore and Ethnomusicology and Director of the Archives of Traditional Music at Indiana University. She has conducted field research on musical performance in West Africa, Saudi Arabia, and Oman, which has been supported by fellowships from Fulbright-Hays, National Endowment for the Humanities, and the Social Science Research Council. Her books include *Let the Inside Be Sweet: An Interpretation of Music Event Among the Kpelle of Liberia* (Bloomington 1982) and *Dried Millet Breaking: Time, Words, and Song in the Woi Epic of the Kpelle* (Bloomington 1988) and co-editor with Frank J. Gillis of *African Oral Data* (Bloomington 1976). She is the First Vice-President of the Society for Ethnomusicology.

CONCILIUM

CONCILIUM

CONCILIUM 1988

All back issues are still in print: available from bookshops (price £5.95) or direct from the publishers (£6.45/US$10.95/Can$12.75 including postage and packing).

T & T CLARK LTD, 59 GEORGE STREET
EDINBURGH EH2 2LQ, SCOTLAND